Eye Contact

*The True Story of a Teenage Jewish Girl
in the Nazi Time*

J.T. Westfield

Copyright © 2022 by J.T. Westfield
All rights reserved

Contents

Prologue		v
Chapter One	"That You Should Die For Something You Know Nothing About"	1
Chapter Two	"Hitler Wants You Jews!"	5
Chapter Three	Forced to Flee Berlin	14
Chapter Four	Time Before the Terror	23
Chapter Five	The Terror Arrives	33
Chapter Six	Hiding Jews in the Attic	43
Chapter Seven	Belgium Gets the Yellow Stars/Mama's Operation	54
Chapter Eight	Alfred Blum/A Round-Up	66
Chapter Nine	"I Cook with Chemistry!"	76
Chapter Ten	The Nazis Count the Children	83
Chapter Eleven	Shopping With Nazis	91
Chapter Twelve	Blum and Marie Albert	99
Chapter Thirteen	Desperation Arrives!	106
Chapter Fourteen	"We'd Love to Take Her…"	116
Chapter Fifteen	A Strange End Sensation	122
Epilogue		129

Prologue

"There is no way I should even be here! I was the little cockroach that skated through…" Helga Wallnau Burch

(Editor's note: Readers and friends, we are indeed blessed and privileged to have this story from Helga Wallnau Burch firsthand. So many other accounts have been lost to time. Her testimony is a vital piece of the Holocaust picture, an eyewitness account from a teenager who lived through it. You'll never read anything quite like it. Helga Wallnau and Anne Frank were the same age, yet Helga's experience is nothing like Anne's. Helga is out there, often perilously confronting Nazis in the streets of occupied Brussels. How she did it is the miracle of this story. Could you or I have done the same? Could any one of us? I invite you to put yourself in Helga's shoes as you read her story. Imagine yourself forced to rely on your wits and bravado just to survive.

This all started when my life partner Shirley let it drop that our friend Helga Burch had "lost her family in the Holocaust". It was 1992. I had just returned from a trip to Avignon, France where I'd seen young men dressed in Nazi garb, with tattoos, swastikas and jackboots. They roamed the streets freely and hung together in thuggish packs. People said they drifted up from Florence, Italy.

I'd been invited to France by a young dance choreographer friend, Andrea Gebhardt, to see her latest presentation.

This turned out to be a silent warning in ballet form. Fascism was back. The three-person cast included two dancers from the Berlin Ballet, a husband and wife. In the piece they wore Nazi trenchcoats and helmets for much of the performance. Andrea herself danced *jeters* and arabesques around them in a silver lame jumpsuit. She clearly conveyed the idea that the Nazis had not accepted defeat but merely morphed into a different look.

Back in Carmel Valley I'd known Helga several years already through Shirley.

When I'd told her about seeing young neo-Nazis in Avignon, Helga said she was not surprised. "It was clear to everyone," she said. "They would not just go away."

"Is it true the Nazis killed your family?" I asked. "You've never mentioned it before."

"Oh, I don't like to talk about it," said Helga. She waved a hand dismissively. "All the stories have been told."

"Not yours," I said. "Were you in hiding? Like Anne Frank?"

"Sometimes, yes. But not all the time. I had many survival points, Jeffrey," she tells me quite matter-of-factly. "I could have been caught and sent to the camps many times. I really don't know how I made it." She pauses a moment in thought. "Poor Anne Frank. She and I, we were nearly the same age."

Helga, at sixty-seven, was still very much full of life and laughter. Her memory perfectly intact. She did not exactly volunteer her story.

I was not family. Not even Jewish, I'd been raised Catholic. We were not related in any direct way. She simply responded to my curiosity as a friend. Helga allowed me to coax the story from her memory, even though there were many times it was obvious she was reluctant.

Helga understood the crucial importance of firsthand Holocaust survival stories. She is the first survivor with whom I'd ever spoken personally. It was like discovering a friend had lived through an unimaginable, unspeakable nightmare. With each session as her memories unfolded, a deep sense of privilege welled up inside me.

One of the very first questions I asked her was, "Do you remember your feelings the first time you heard the words, Adolph Hitler?"

To my astonishment, Helga leans back and laughs heartily. "The first time I heard this name 'Adolph Hitler' and was old enough to understand, I loved this man!" She laughed again, then noticed the surprise on my face. "Adolph Hitler got rid of the maid who used to beat me with a cat-of-nine-tails. Do you know what that is?" I nodded. "For nothing really!" she goes on. "For talking back or some little thing. I could never believe my parents allowed this to happen. Well this maid was a Christian. And Hitler had passed laws that said Christians could not work for Jews. But she wrote a letter to Hitler personally. She told him she loved working for my father and she begged Hitler to let her keep her job. She got a letter back from the Reichstag telling her if she didn't quit this job immediately she would be arrested!"

Helga laughed again. "She had to quit. The horrible maid! I loved Hitler for that." She paused, a mischievous twinkle in her eyes. "So you see? Everything is not so simple."

A moment later she resumes.

"My father died in the camps," she says flatly. "My Aunt Frieda too. And my Uncle Walter."

"How did you survive?" I asked now utterly fascinated.

She laughs. Her composed face dissolves and her bright hazel eyes shine with mischief. "I honestly don't know, Jeffrey. By all rights I should be dead." She laughs again. "I was the little cockaroach (sic) that skated through." Her voice rings with glee.

(Editor's note: Helga is well over ninety today and the last we spoke she told me her mind has "gone on vacation". I tease her gently and say, "Wait till you get the bill." Sadly it is true, Helga has forgotten most of her story. "It's up to you, Jeffrey, to remember. I know now why I told it all to you.")

"When did you get out of Berlin?" I asked. "How did you escape Germany?"

"Y'know I did some work in the schools here?" she digresses, referring to the Carmel/Monterey area. "I went and told my story. That was years ago. They were so sweet, those children." Her eyes go misty. "They wrote me thank you notes."

Helga Wallnau Burch loves life. She is a poet. You hear this in her voice and see it in her eyes. She was married here in the U.S. and had two sons. Her poems have won awards. She is also a psychologist with a degree in Marriage and Family Counseling. Helga has none of the bitterness many Holocaust survivors express. The "why did I survive?" complex. She reads and admires all the Holocaust memoirists like Primo Levi and Etty Hillesum. Helga was also invited to share her story with the Yale University Holocaust Archives.

Helga Wallnau aged 15

Chapter One

"That You Should Die For Something You Know Nothing About"

Most of Helga's story will be told in basic chronological order. However, we begin with this one encounter, from the middle of the story, as an introduction to Helga Wallnau, the teenager. It was also the first episode of her ordeal which she related to me. This "survival point" as she called it, occurred in Brussels, Belgium in the spring 1942 almost two years after she and her mother had escaped Berlin.

'I guess I was about sixteen,' said Helga. 'This particular evening, I met my friend Ruth from school, as we'd made a plan to go to the movies together. The theater was a little more than a mile from where my mother and I lived in Brussels, Belgium.

'We'd fled from the Nazis in Berlin," she went on. "And now they'd followed us to Belgium. My mother made sure that I wore the hideous yellow star on my nice coat. But I had a large square handbag that I wore high on my shoulder. Like this!' She demonstrates with a sly smile. 'The handbag covered up that ugly star. When the movie finished, I said goodbye to my friend Ruth. She was a half-Christian girl, and she lived close by, but in the opposite direction.

Ruth suggested I come stay at her house as it was almost curfew.

"Oh no," I told her. "My mother would worry herself sick. I'll be all right."

Ruth gave me a hug and left. It was then I noticed the man in the black coat watching me. He was SS. He came up and spoke to me in German.'

"Where is your star?" he demanded. This man is Gestapo, I know, but he shows me nothing himself. No badge or I.D

"Right here," I say, moving my handbag aside to show the awful star.

"Why do you hide it? I could arrest you just for that, you know?"

I say nothing at first and think of my mother, if she should find out I am arrested. Then I say, "It's so ugly on my nice coat. That's why I hide it." This Gestapo is a very handsome young German. Deep blue eyes and blond hair cut short. From his accent I can tell he is 'Ausland Deutsche' that is, German from the countryside.

"Do you know there is a curfew for Jews after eight o'clock? Where do you live?"

I tell him the address of my mother's friend where we are living.

"That is over one kilometer from here, you cannot possibly get home before the curfew," he informs me. "And I see that you do not walk so well."

"I walk well enough. I will be home on time." This Gestapo is only a few years older than I. He is very highly trained. A German boy who can speak Hebrew and Yiddish both.

He says, "I could arrest you or even shoot you! And I would get a special medal for this. Do you realize that? It would be a big plus for my career. Do you understand that? I could shoot you!"

I nod and answer, "Yes." But all this time I am searching his eyes. To make contact with the human being underneath all the training and the brainwash. Eye contact! It was always like that. You had to reach the human element in their soul. Your life depended on it.

"You are Jewish," he says. "You wear the star. Although you hide it. Do you speak Hebrew?"

I shake my head no.

"Do you know the Torah?"

Again I shake my head no.

"Do you have any idea what it means to be Jewish?"

"No," I reply.

We look at one another for a time. Then he says, "Isn't it sad that you should die for something you know nothing about?" The words are horrific, but there is little fire behind them I can tell. Spoken more like general information rather than a threat.

I say nothing now. Just wait. And hold eye contact with this man.

At last he tells me to go. Get home as quickly as I can. And don't get caught out again after curfew. That was one of the very bad moments for me. And as I realize later, it was a survival point.

'Survival points', Helga calls them. Run-ins with Nazis, that is. Any one of which could have and should have spelled the end for Helga, and bought her a one-way train ticket to Auschwitz. It's one miraculous escape after another which she relates to me in various sessions over the course of a year or so. Often times she tells the same story over, enlightening me with a different nuance or context. Psychological factors would often come out later in our discussions. It was always the psychology behind the encounters which most intrigued us both.

"Do you remember this young Gestapo at all?' I ask. 'Do you have any idea why he let you go?"

"Oh yes! I remember him very well. He was handsome. Not much older than me." She considers a moment. "We don't know exactly why he let me go. Not really. Maybe he felt sorry for me? That I was so out of it!" She laughs a high lilting laugh. "We can only suppose that I reached his soul somehow. I held eye contact with them always. I don't even know why. Something told me to do that. If you look at each other long enough, you find the common humanity you share. Something like that."

"Maybe he was attracted to you a little?"

"No, no." Helga insists. "These men were trained against such feelings. It was all part of their education in the SS. They were taught Hebrew and Yiddish. And they studied the Torah. This man knew what it meant to be Jewish, even if I didn't."

I grimaced. "Yeah, it meant he could shoot you!" I said. Helga's irony could be devastating. "So? How did you come to be in Brussels? When did you leave Berlin?"

"I will tell you. I will tell you everything…"

Chapter Two

"Hitler Wants You Jews!"

"So, your Uncle Erich got out? With his family? When did they leave?" I asked Helga. "Why didn't you guys all leave together?"

"Uncle Paul was the first to leave," said Helga. "He left very early. From Munich. He saw Hitler in the beerhalls! Paul was my father's younger brother. He fled to Zurich, where he met a family who at first, even offered to take me in."

(Editor's note: Helga's family story was brimming with sex and scandal. Her mother's mother had come from money but had married a Hungarian gypsy and thus been disinherited. Helga relates it all with much glee and high spirits. Her father Hans Wallnau had two brothers, one younger, Paul, and one older, Walter. In a picture she shows me from 1925, all three brothers wear impeccable suits, sharp ties and stiff collars.

Paul Wallnau (above) has a rounder, gentler face and wears spectacles. He'd been living in Munich when Hitler came up rousing the rabble in the beerhalls against Jews. Blaming them for all Germany's problems. Paul worked as a theater director. And also a performer. He couldn't stomach the Nazis and he moved to Zurich in '34. There he became a theater director for the biggest musical theater in town. His fiancée was a Steiner, from a fabulously wealthy Zurich family who owned the theater, where Paul was now director. Early on the Steiner Family offered to take Helga in, to keep her safe.

But when the Steiner fiancée learned of Paul Wallnau's fondness for carousing around town, she threw herself in the Zurich Lake. That scotched the plans to shelter Helga. And it hindered Paul's career for some years afterwards.)

"What about your father?" I ask. "Didn't he see it was time to leave?"

"Oh," Helga scoffs. "My father believed Hitler couldn't last. Uncle Paul and Uncle Erich knew better. They got out. Uncle Erich was my mother's oldest brother. And he had loaned my father a lot of money for his business. My father was a dreamer. He had these plans for an inexpensive men's suit. Three pieces with a vest, y'know? There was nothing affordable like it anywhere at the time. It was an innovation for the working-class man. My father believed in such things. That men should try to better their appearance, that it was related to their self-esteem."

The picture Helga paints of their time in Berlin before they had to flee is right out of the movie "Cabaret". Pure Weimar Republic! I asked if she knew the movie?

"Oh yes! It made me think of my dear Aunt Tigla," Helga goes on. "And her beautiful daughter, Magda. They lived in a giant house with many rooms across town from us in Berlin. They would rent out rooms to professors and the like. Just like in the film. I loved to visit Aunt Tigla. When she spoke, her teeth went up and down, up and down." Helga holds her finger in front of her mouth and wags it several times. Then she laughs. "Often I would ride the streetcar across the city to see her and Magda." She pauses. "I remember the name of one gentleman who lived there, Herr Aussipoff!" And she laughs.

Helga was a gifted storyteller. She paints scenes and incidents vividly and deftly. Much of the pre-survival story sounded right out of the pages of Christopher Isherwood and "The Berlin Diaries" which eventually became the movie "Cabaret".

Helga laughs gleefully.

"So?" I ask. "Was it as wild as they say before Hitler? Berlin and the whole cabaret scene?"

"Well, I was only a child." Helga smiles with a twinkle of delight in her eyes. "But one night I did see my father pour champagne into my mother's bathtub."

I laughed. "Really?"

"Yes! And my Uncle Erich? My mother's older brother. He had two mistresses. At the same time! He kept them both in a big gorgeous flat in a fancy part of Berlin. And he drove all around Berlin in a Bentley and a Rolls Royce. Two big fancy cars."

"You met his mistresses?"

"Oh no! I learned everything from my Aunt Frieda. She knew everything and she told my mother everything. I was always eavesdropping.

"Erich's mistresses were both quite beautiful," Helga continues. "One was ash blond and the other was a beautiful brunette. They were both Christian. Hitler would force my uncle to give them up." She pauses. "But my parents had affairs too. You have to understand before my mother married my father, she had many men chasing after her. Some of them very wealthy. My mother was very beautiful. And intelligent."

"What about your Uncle Erich? He couldn't convince your father to leave?"

"My father was Prussian! Very stubborn! Erich was more a man of the world. He had started out shining shoes. And become a millionaire! My father was different. He came from the upper middle class. His father was a well-known photographer. My grandfather used to send me birthday cakes. Every year! With little chocolate mice, a mouse for each year. He made a scandal by marrying their beautiful housemaid after my grandmother died."

"So?" I asked. "Not everyone escaped then?"

"No. Uncle Walter didn't want to leave. He was my father's older brother."

Walter Wallnau's problems were financial. He worked in stocks and bonds and had been basically wiped out in the downturn of 1929. Walter always needed money. Helga recalled one day he showed up at their apartment and said to her father, "So? How's my credit standing in this house?"

Helga's father Hans threw his older brother out of the apartment. But Helga's mother Elka, secretly gave Walter cash behind her husband's back. Walter would end up refusing to leave Berlin. He would die in the camps and many years later get a commemorative stone in the sidewalk. A tribute modern Germans paid to the many Germans killed in the Holocaust.

Elka's sister Frieda Oling would also refuse to leave.

Helga says, "I learned everything from my Aunt Freida. What she didn't tell me directly I got from eavesdropping. Freida lived quite nearby and she was always over at our apartment. She and my mother were very close. Freida handled all the money for Uncle Erich's business. And there was a lot of it. She was his bookkeeper. But she never liked my father. She was always running him down to my mother. 'That husband of yours, such a poor head for business', she'd say.

"Aunt Freida would take me out for breakfast to a swank hotel. She would point out one couple or another and tell me if they were married or not. When I asked how she knew, she said, 'You can tell the married ones. The husband reads the paper and has nothing to say to his wife. If they're not married, they always have a lot to talk about'." Helga laughs.

"Freida taught me a lot. She taught me everything. She had a bad leg like mine and she always said, 'Never let it stop you, Helga! Live your life like it's a normal leg, like everyone else's.' Uncle Erich tried to get Freida to leave and come to New York with them. But she had a Christian boyfriend there in Berlin and she wouldn't leave him. Erich gave her a diamond as big as your thumb before he left." Helga pauses a moment. "Freida died in the camps. The diamond obviously didn't save her."

*

Helga recounts the story of Erich's farewell get-together in Berlin at her Uncle's beautiful house. Fancy furniture. The requisite set of beer steins on wall, small to large. She describes Uncle Erich as not terribly big or broad-shouldered, but wiry, boisterous and very full of life and energy. For his second wife he'd married a woman named Molly and they had a daughter named Marion. "I didn't like Marion much," Helga told me. "She was so bossy. My mother would always ask if I want to go play with Cousin Marion and I would always say no."

I asked why Uncle Erich had married Molly?

"Erich had been married before," Helga relates. "He'd come home one day and found his first wife in bed with a lover. He sent her on a world cruise and divorced her. Then he married Molly a few years later. Jewish. With connections in the Berlin bureaucracy. She would help when they needed visas.

"Aunt Molly had beautiful china and silver flatware. At her dinner parties she served the tiniest portions. Each one on a different plate, as if it were a restaurant in Paris. During one such dinner my father had teased, 'So Molly? When are we actually going to eat?' Aunt Molly never forgave him for that.

"At this last reunion party everyone was there from my mother's family. Uncle Erich went around to all his nieces and nephews. He would look at us up close and say, 'Have you been good? Do you sing in the choir?' Then he would laugh at the look on your face.

"Uncle Martin had come with his wife and children. And Uncle Josi, who was the only real practicing Jew in the family and his son Bernie. Of course Aunt Frieda was there and even Uncle Walter Wallnau too, my father's older brother. He always wore silk stockings, Uncle Walter. Even though he had no money. Walter loved sweet potatoes and when I took the last one from the platter, he leaned over to me and said, 'Child, you should learn what it means to be hungry'." Helga pauses. "I've never forgotten that. Uncle Walter was something."

"That day Uncle Karl Oling and his teenage son had come from Austria. I'd never met Karl before, only heard of him. I think he was in the middle of the four Oling brothers and two sisters. We'd heard Karl had fallen in with followers of Madame Blavatsky, who'd help form Nazism. The conversation during the dinner included much talk of Hitler and the Nazis.

"Uncle Erich told his favorite story from World War I. How he'd surprised another soldier in the dead of night separated by a thick hedge of shrubbery. Just before they shot, Erich called out, 'Hey? Are you a Yid?' Meaning are you Jewish? When the enemy soldier, replied, 'Yeah, are you?' 'Yah!' Erich had called back and the two soldiers stood up and embraced.

"My father Hans told the story of finding another 'Wallnau' in the new phone directory. '…When I called him up?' said Hans. 'He was very warm and friendly. And also surprised. We figured out we must be second or third cousins. When I suggested we meet for a beer on Wednesday, he said, 'No, I have the Party Meeting that day'. Then he asked if I was in the Party? I said, 'No, I'm Jewish.' Then he called me 'a dirty Jew' and said to never call him again." My father laughed. Everyone laughed. Except Uncle Karl and his son.

"Uncle Erich and my father had both earned the Iron Cross in World War I. All during the dinner Karl and his son both talk up how the Nazis are good for Germany and lifting-up the economy and such. Uncle Erich tries to tell them that Hitler means to destroy them and all things Jewish. 'Why do you think we're leaving? I've been ordered to close my business!' He talks about the camps that are being filled with dissenters. The anti-Jewish laws! Things get very tense at the table.

"All of a sudden, Uncle Karl's teenage son stands up and says, 'What's the matter with you people? Hitler doesn't want us, he only wants you Jews!" And he points an ugly finger at poor Uncle Josi and Cousin Bernie who sat there with their yarmulkes on their heads.

At that point Uncle Erich stands up and shouts at Karl, "Get out! Get out of my house right now, Karl! You and your son! Both of you! Get out!"

Editor's note: Almost two years later in November of 1938 Berlin experiences mass riots in the street, what would later be called Kristallnacht! The Night of Broken Glass.

Kristallnacht was sparked by a dissident Jew shooting a low-level German Nazi bureaucrat (the victim, according to Helga, a distant cousin of her Uncle Erich's libidinous first wife). The incident touches off several days of anti-Jewish riots across all of Germany. The shooter was a young Jew whose parents had been deported. Riots, murders, arrests and vast destruction of Jewish businesses followed. Overnight Berlin sidewalks are covered in broken storefront glass. Hence the phrase, *Kristalnacht*! Night of Broken Glass. Any business with a Jewish sounding name was destroyed.

Helga's surname "Wallnau" is not so obviously Jewish. Her father Hans Wallnau's small clothing manufacturing shop is not touched. Two days later however a couple of Nazi SS come snooping around the office building looking for a "Hans Wallnau".

"Why were you still in Berlin in '38?" I ask. "Wasn't it late already?"

Helga says, "Oh! My father always said, Hitler can't last! He must've said it a thousand times. Two days after the riots my father finally realizes he must leave. He travels to Holland, where he is instantly put into a relocation camp with thousands of other Germans all fleeing the Nazis. My mother was left behind to tend to the business. She connected with a Christian man, a friend of my father, who agreed to 'manage' things till this Nazi stuff was over. Jews could no longer own any business. That was the law."

"So, how long did you stay in Berlin? After your father left?"

"About a month or two," she says. "Then we had to leave. It was, like you say, almost too late. Our life in Berlin was over. My father coming home from work for dinner. Then going out to his club to read the papers. Playing Souza marches on the small piano in our hallway. Over forever."

(Editor's note: Helga relates her experiences 'during the Nazi time' as she calls it over a period of months. Some of it we record on videotape. She tells short vignettes most always out of chronological order, little incidents, which illuminate very precise moral shadings. The basic elements of each episode never vary no matter how often she tells it. And that in turn bears out the essential truth of her story as a whole.

It fell upon me to organize and present her testimony in a cohesive manner. As our sessions continued and more details emerged, my amazement grew with each interview. This adolescent girl had flummoxed the entire Third Reich!

There's a complex psychological core to Helga's story. Aside from the drama and suspense, there's the ever-present question of motivation. What moved people to act the way they did? Both Nazis and the Non-Nazis. Was it fear? Anger? Spite? The ones who helped and the ones who didn't. Can we, in this time today, even understand how treacherous, how dangerous her life became during the Nazi time?

Among those who helped Helga survive, some would later be charged with collaboration after the war. Few were convicted. The main question lies in the very personal nature of resistance to autocratic tyranny. How much are any of us willing to risk? The fact that Helga Wallnau, like Anne Frank, is a teenager is also crucial to her story. The world we experience as teenagers is not the same world we inhabit as adults. Anne lives and resists through her diary. Helga survives but her story is dual edged. On one side is the resistance and on the other collaboration. That is the crux of it for us, as well. Many Holocaust researchers feel it was more traumatic the younger you were, because adults are better equipped mentally to deal with adult treachery. We leave that call to the reader.

We will fill in some details of Helga's family later in the history, her father Hans Wallnau and his two brothers Paul and Walter, and her mother Elka Oling Wallnau and Elka's sister Frieda Oling and their four brothers. But let's start with Helga and her mother's escape from Germany in January of 1939. Helga was thirteen. Born with a bad leg, she'd suffered numerous surgeries to fix it. None of them quite worked. She would endure a limp for her entire life, though I never heard her complain about it. Ever!

Elka Oling Wallnau circa 1938

Eye Contact

Chapter Three

Forced to Flee Berlin

'That morning the phone in our Berlin apartment, it rang and rang and rang. My mother did not want to answer. My father had been gone several months already. Put into a refugee camp in Holland. We'd gotten one letter. My mother stood there in the kitchen watching the phone ring. I knew she was in there. Why didn't she pick it up?

I called out, "Mama! The phone! Mama?"

It was a nice apartment we had, near Fredrichstrasse in the better part of Berlin. It was full of beautiful things and was quite comfortable to live in.

When my mother finally does pick up the phone, the conversation is brief. "Yah?"

The voice on the other end recited a password. These passwords came from the underground, the resistance. My mother recites the proper response. The voice then gives her an address in the border town of Aachen and another password to use there, along with the proper response. My mother writes this all down. The voice says goodbye and good luck. My mother says thank you and hangs up the phone. She looks closely at what she's written. She memorizes it. Then she takes the piece of paper over to the sink, puts a kitchen match to it and washes the ashes down the drain.

I was arranging things in my little weekender bag when she came into my room. She hugged me close before she said anything. "We're leaving today, Liebchen. Our train is in two hours."

"I'm all packed and ready, Mama. Look!"

"Oh Helga-chen, my love! We take only our pocketbooks today. No suitcase. I want you to wear two sweaters under your good winter coat. A light one first over your blouse, then a heavy one on top of that. Put a pair of underwear in your purse along with your toothbrush and hairbrush. It must look like a short trip. That is the key."

I nod. "Okay, mama." I was already thirteen. But I really didn't get it. That we were running for our lives. Maybe I never really got it? The whole time.

'The train ride from Berlin to Aachen, near the Belgian border took several hours. None of our fellow passengers looked scared or on the run, but undoubtedly many were. Just like us.

We arrived in Aachen as night fell. Outside the station we found a taxi. My mother gave him the address and he studied us both for a long moment. When we arrive at the address, the cab driver refuses to take any money. He drops us and speeds off before my mother can pay him.

'It was an old brownstone, like you see in New York, a large building with a common entrance. We climb the steps to the front door. My mother knocks. No one comes. She knocks again. And again. Finally we hear footsteps come shuffling towards the door. It opens a tiny crack to reveal an elderly man.

My mother recites the password. The old man seems not to hear. Mother recites the password again. Again the old man looks confused. He closes the door.

We stood there a long while before the door opened again.

This time it was a woman about my mother's age. My mother repeats the password. The woman gives the proper response.

"Welcome, welcome!" she gushes as she introduces herself. "I'm sorry about my father. He was the man you saw. He gets confused about it all. Still." This woman was truly warm and nice. My mother introduces us and we all shake hands.

When she lets us inside, I don't believe what I see! The room is like Grand Central Station at the rush hour. A madhouse! All sorts of people, families and couples and singles all with bags and trunks and suitcases. They cluster and huddle in close quiet nervousness. They speak in whispers or just sit there saying nothing at all.

It was amazing! From the outside you could tell nothing.

The nice woman comes up to us again. "Have you arranged to meet a guide?"

My mother says, "No. I have no contacts here in Aachen. Just a little money."

The nice woman nods. She looks concerned. "Well there's a guide over there who's been waiting for a man from Hamburg. The man is very late. Two or three hours now. Let me talk to him a moment." And she left us. I saw her go speak to a middle-aged man who was dressed as if he were about to take an Alpine hike. His boots looked worn but durable.

A few minutes later my mother is talking with this man, whose name is Frischal. He tells my mother his usual method of transport is to board the westbound train in Aachen. This train winds its way uphill as it crosses into Belgian territory for several miles before crossing back into Germany. Frischal and his emigres leap from the slow-moving train as it passes through Belgium. Nazi soldiers placed on the train to prevent such things will fire on the fleeing figures, but Frischal says, "They don't really want to kill us. I think they fire over our heads. Just for show."

Elka nods. "Yah, well this is okay for me. I can jump from a train. But my daughter Helga, she has had many operations on her leg. I don't think this will work for her."

Frischal looks over at me. "I understand. There is another way maybe for young Helga here. I have some friends who might be able to help." His friends, he says, live in Belgium but work at construction jobs here in Aachen, on the German side of the border. They cross back and forth every day. "But," he adds. "They all have identity papers. We'll have to find some papers for Helga. Let me telephone."

Frischal disappears for some time. When he returns he looks doubtful. "Well, they are all for helping out. And they have some papers for a teenaged girl. But she looks nothing like your Helga."

My mother nods. "So what do we do?"

"Well," Frischal says thoughtfully. "She simply keeps her head down. When the border guard asks to see her face, she claims she is too drunk to lift her head. She says she will vomit if she lifts her head and she simply keeps her head down. No matter what happens, she does not lift her face up." He looks back and forth from my mother to me. "Can you do this? Can you play act that you're so drunk you can't lift your head?"

Helga nods quickly. "I'm a good actress," I tell him. "I can do this. No matter what, I do not lift up my head."

"Yah, okay. That's a good girl then." Frischal turns back to Elka. "How much do you have?" He meant money, but I had no idea how much my mother had.

Mother turns away from me and talks to Frischal in a whisper. Frischal looks troubled but eventually he nods. "Well my original prospect has not turned up, so I will do this for you and your daughter for what you have. Even though my regular fee is much higher than that."

'My mother had turned him, I understood that. Mother was very beautiful. She had such an effect on men. Style, class and a figure to match. That was my mother! All her life she'd had what her sister Frieda called "admirers". I knew for a fact she'd been courted by the heir to the Farbin steel fortune. I could never understand exactly what she saw in my father. But this guide Mr. Frischal had been charmed. My mother was wonderful that way.

'As we leave the safe house however, Frischal's original client, the man from Hamburg, comes running up the sidewalk. He spoke the password still catching his breath. "I am so sorry to be late. My train was delayed."

"Yes, I understand," says Frischal. "But now I've made a contract with this lady from Berlin. And her daughter. I can't just drop them."

The man from Hamburg looks very upset.

Frischal then says, "It's more risk. But I take you both. Come on."

Hamburg smiles. "I'll pay you extra for the risk." He too, I could tell right off, was intrigued by my mother.

At that moment a small sedan bearing four Belgian workers pulls up to the curb. This was my ride.

My mother hugs me fiercely. "Be brave, my darling! Keep your head down. I love you!"

"Don't worry Mama!" I hug her back. "Everything will be fine." I climb into the car. It reeks of human sweat and schnapps. These guys are a rough sort. Blue collar type. They work hard for a living, I could tell. As we drive they offer me a sip from the bottle. When I shake my head no, they insist.

"For the guards," one worker tells me. "At the border. Your breath!"

I understand and I take a sip of the schnapps. It burns my throat. I was in the back seat between two Belgians as we roll up to the border crossing. It was dark. These Belgian guys had started singing loud bawdy songs. I try to sing too, though I do not know the songs.

It was completely dark outside. The only light comes from inside the small guard shack. Two Nazi border guards approach the car, one on each side.

The Belgian driver rolls down his window and hands the identity papers out. Then the passenger in front opens his window and hands out papers including the one for me. The guard studies my paper. He motions for the Belgian beside me to roll down the window.

"Lift your head, Fraulein! So I can see your face!"

"No, no, I can't!" I cry, keeping my head down. "I'll be sick! I will vomit! Too much schnapps!"

"Come on! Just one moment! Look up here."

"No! No! I'm sick!"

At that moment the other Belgian guy beside me gets out of the car and looks as if he's about to urinate. He pretends to be very very drunk.

"Hey!" shouts the other guard. "What do you think you're doing there? You Belge pig!"

"What? I can't pee here?" says the Belgian. Then he sings, "Don't pee here!"

Meanwhile the guard on our side is distracted by all this, but only for a moment. "Fraulein! Look over here at me!" He still holds my identity paper.

"No!" I keep my head down. "I am sick! I will vomit! On my good coat!"

"You!" the other guard shouts at the Belgian pretending to pee. "Get back in the car or I arrest you! Right now!" Then he calls out to the other guard. "Get rid of this swine!"

"They've got a drunk girl in the back seat here."

"Yah, that figures all right. Let them have her!" He turns back. "Achtung! You Belgian swine! Get the hell out of here! Now!"

The guard on our side shrugs and hands back the papers. We drive across. Some distance away, the Belgians stop for a moment. They congratulate me on my performance and they start to drink again. I cannot tell if they were frightened at all. Or if it was more like a game to them. Belgians versus Germans. They were thrilled to have out-foxed those border guards. The Belgians had risked their lives for me, a complete stranger. It was amazing!

Train Station Aachen, Germany. cir. 1939

'Meanwhile my mother Elka, Herr Frischal the guide, and the man from Hamburg play out a different charade on the train. This is the westbound train out of Aachen. They all three pretend to meet in the bar car, where they enjoy a friendly cocktail. Hamburg proceeds to chat up my mother and she in turn acts as if she might be interested. The barman makes conversation with Frischal. And Frischal in turn tells the barman he wishes he had "the wallet" to pursue such a woman like Elka there.

"She looks married if you ask me," says the barman.

Frischal gives him a leer. "All the better then, right?"

"Ah! You're a devil!" The barman laughs.

Hamburg lights a cigarette and then lights one for Elka. They are talking low, when two Nazi soldiers come into the car. They carry rifles on their shoulders. They give them all a once-over look and proceed out the back. The barman tells Hamburg they can only smoke in the next car up. Elka and Hamburg leave. Frischal follows a minute later.

In the smoking car there is an emergency exit door. A large woman clutching a small dog stands nearby and puffs nervously on a cigarette. She pretends not to notice my mother and Hamburg, who appear to be engrossed in each other. Frischal enters and smiles at the woman. The dog barks and she quiets it. Then she sizes up Frischal and starts right in telling him about being on this same train last week, right here in this car when someone threw open the emergency door and leaped out.

"You don't say, Madam!" says Frischal. He lights up a cigarette. "Damn Jews! They scurry like rats nowadays."

"Yes, most likely," the woman answers. "Personally though, I prefer them to the Communists." She snugs the little dog under her chin and makes baby talk to it.

"Oh yes!" says Frischal. "Though many are one and the same of course. But then I know many good Jews who fought hard for Germany in the Great War."

"Of course, of course!" says the woman trying not to stare at Hamburg and Elka. From the looks of their clothes they made a stylish couple. "But why must they jump off the train like that? Quite unnerves my dog!"

"Indeed madam!" Frischal commiserates. "Indeed!"

The train slows as it starts uphill. It's barely going five miles per hour. Frischal suddenly grabs the handle of the emergency door and throws it open. The woman makes a shout. The dog yipes and nearly jumps out of her arms. She falls back clutching the animal tightly. Frischal urges Hamburg up to the open door. It's pitch black outside, the dark landscape sweeps by.

"Go!" shouts Frischal to Hamburg who hesitates. "Now!"

Hamburg leaps off the train. The woman screams in earnest now, dog barking in her arms. Frischal sweeps his arm around my mother's waist lifts her up and together they leap into the black nothingness. The woman's fading screams give way to the sound of rifle fire. But no bullets come anywhere near them.

*

Helga continued, 'I was driven many miles into the countryside with my new Belgian friends. I spent a sleepless night in a lovely cottage, where they fed me and tucked me into a lovely bed with a down quilt. Worry for my mother kept me wide awake.

Sometime before dawn the woman of the house enters the room and says, "Come child, we go find your mother now."

And out into the dark forest we go. We walk and walk for close to an hour. As dawn breaks, the trees all begin to look like human figures and I keep peering out and thinking, "There! There is my mother!" But it wasn't. It was only another bare tree.

Then finally, we hear voices! One of the shadows turns out to be my mother. But oh! She looks terrible! Like I've never seen before! Her beautiful clothes are dirty and torn. Her wonderful shoes are tied together with string.

"Oh mama! Mama!" I am crying as she hugs me close.

"It's okay Helga-chen! I am here." My mother is bone weary. You hear it in her voice. They've been walking through the Belgian forest all night. Frischal and Hamburg look almost as bad.

Belgium was still free at this time. The next day we catch the train to Brussels where we find the address of my cousin Bernie, Uncle Josi's son. Bernie was about eighteen or so, Uncle Josi's only son. Josi was one of my mother's four brothers. Bernie was a tailor by trade and he was actually working. Later on I heard he even sewed Nazi uniforms. It's possible. I don't know, but I wouldn't have blamed him.

My mother and I stay with him for a very short time until we find a place of our own.

Chapter Four

Time Before the Terror

(Editor's note: Helga's story has me hooked by this time. Following each session I can hardly wait to hear more.)

I asked how they managed in Brussels after they arrived, she and her mother?

Helga says, 'When we arrive at the address of my cousin Bernie, he's been living there in Brussels for some time. Three months back, in Berlin, his father Joseph Oling, had received his "pink slip" in the mail.

Like so many others it told him to report to the local police station to be "registered". When Josi went, he was arrested on the spot. When Bernie went to try to find him, he was arrested as well. Father and son were eventually put on the same train to the camps. When the Nazis made them switch trains in the middle of the night, Bernie slipped away into the forest. He'd hitchhiked for two days to reach Brussels.

How hard it must've been for Bernie to leave his father, I said.

Helga tells me it was hard for everyone.

I ask how Bernie learned tailoring. She tells me Josi had been a tailor and had taught Bernie as he'd grown up. Helga and her mother stay on with Bernie a few nights. Then Helga finds them a place, one of the very few without bed bugs. "Every place in Brussels had bed bugs," she says. "All over!"

Ironically there was no heat either.

Still it would carry them through the warm spring and summer. On a walk through their nice neighborhood Helga spots a beautiful big school with ornate sculpting on the exterior.

'It was a Catholic school taught by the nuns,' says Helga. 'And I beg my mother to let me go there. So my mother goes to see the Mother Superior and they have an interview. Now my mother speaks very little Flemish. The nuns speak no German. Yet somehow my mother gets it over that I love everything Catholic and had once even fantasized about being a nun. They must've had a good laugh over that one. But they agree to let me in their school. Oh! How I loved every day there. I just adored those nuns.

'When I asked my mother how she talked them into it? She laughed and said she had no idea, none whatsoever! My mother told me she wasn't sure they'd understood a word she said. But oh! I was overjoyed to go to that school with those nuns. I loved them all! I remember them to this day.'

It was after dropping Helga at school that her mother Elka would stop into a café in the neighborhood for a coffee and a glance at the newspapers. She couldn't bear to read much, it made her heart ache for her husband Hans. Most every night of their married life he'd gone to his club after dinner to smoke and read the papers. He'd loved to play the piano as well. Marches! He played Souza and Stephen Foster so beautifully.

Elka Oling, Helga's mother, had been a mere girl when her brother Erich first brought Hans Wallnau to their house. He'd played piano and Elka had sung along. She'd liked Hans and he'd been charmed by her. But once she'd come of age Elka had been pursued by many wealthy suitors, most of them business associates of Erich's. Clothing manufacture was the family's line of business. Elka had studied briefly in Paris and discovered an immense talent for fashion design. In fact she could draw patterns from memory, having only seen the finished product. So it was only after some years that Elka and Hans Wallnau decided to marry. Elka liked it that Hans was a bit of a socialist. He believed in capitalism but still thought the average guy should get a break.

They'd gotten a few letters from him here in Brussels. Hans Wallnau was still in a Dutch internment camp. In the café this afternoon Elka was rereading one of the letters when she heard her name.

"Elka?" said a tall thin woman holding a coffee. "Elka Wallnau? Is that you?"

Elka looks up but does not recognize the woman immediately.

"It's me, Erna Unghar! Remember? I met you in Berlin with my Harry. He's old friends with your husband Hans. We all went to the cabaret together? Oh my Lord! You're more beautiful than ever, my dear. What are you doing here in Brussels? Harry will be delighted to see Hans."

Elka remembers the woman now. "Yes, yes, I remember. How are you, Erna?"

The place was nearly empty at this hour well after lunch. Besides the bartender and the waiter there were only a couple of businessmen with female companions.

"Oh!" Erna exclaims. "We're preparing for the worst, Harry and I. Everyone knows that bastard Hitler is bent on taking over all of Europe. What about you and Hans?"

Elka shows her the letter postmarked Camp Westerbrook in Holland. She tells Erna a brief account of their escape from Germany.

"Oh, you poor dears!" Erna sympathizes. "And Helga with her bad foot and all? Oh my God! Someone should shoot that bastard Adolph! How old is your Helga now?"

"Almost fourteen. She's very strong. We keep each other going." The waiter brings them two fresh coffees and tells them it's on the house. He knows parts of Elka's story. "You and Harry are married then?" Elka asks.

"No, no not yet!" Erna laughs. "But we're planning on it. Soon. He's trying to get all his investments out of Germany. He knows Hitler will nationalize everything. How are you getting along?"

"I brought what money I could. Hans arranged for a Christian friend of ours to run the business in Berlin. He's supposed to send money. But so far, nothing."

"Hitler needs every pfennig for tanks, I wouldn't count on him letting too much money out of the country." Erna smiles brightly. "You and Helga must come to dinner tonight. Harry will be so delighted to see you. He misses Berlin terribly." And she gives Elka a conspiratorial wink. "He says, 'Brussels is so boring! No night life to speak of'."

*

When Elka and Helga show up at Erna's large flat they encounter Harry outside on the stoop. He says, "Hello, hello! Erna is doing the floors inside, we must stay out here until the polish dries." He gives them an embarrassed grin.

Elka smiles, "So nice to see you again, Harry. This is my daughter Helga." They all shake hands. Harry was Jewish, but very handsome. Helga says, 'He had blue eyes like Paul Newman. And he was tall and blond. He was the type that every woman falls for head over heels. Quite successful in business too. He and my father had been friends a long time.'

"I admire you and Hans for hanging on as long as you did," says Harry as he carves up a small roast at Erna's dinner table. "We all kept hoping Germany would wake up in time. Before Adolph and his fascists got too powerful. Now it's as if all of Germany has fallen under his spell." Harry deftly doles out slices of meat. "I'm not too worried for Erna here. She doesn't have any Yids hanging off her family tree. But if that bastard Adolph conquers Europe he's going to try to round up every last one of us. I'm certain of that."

Elka nods and passes a plate to Helga. There is much more food than they are used to seeing. Potatoes and vegetables and meat galore.

"Enough, Harry!" Erna gestures. "You'll frighten them half to death!" Erna had been a fashion model in her younger days.

Still thin as a rail, she had big eyes, rather like Bette Davis. "Can't we talk of something else?"

Helga recalls, 'Erna intimidated me with those big eyes. She no longer looked like a model. She was plain now. But there was a force to her. She was a Christian woman. Not terribly bright. And too honest, if you know what I mean. She pushed Harry away, always scrubbing her floors, day and night. She was nothing cozy to come home to, I'll tell you. That honesty of hers, it came out too much.'

'After that first night my mother and I began eating dinner there two or three times a week. I developed a crush on Harry, who would often walk us back home to our loft apartment. Harry was so handsome! And his clothes were always the best. Of course I noticed the way he looked at my mother. But then most men looked at my mother that way. With obvious desire. Mother always had her "admirers" as Aunt Freida called them. You could hardly blame Harry, as Erna kept herself as plain as shortening bread.

'My mother asked me once if I hoped my future husband would look like Harry?'

I told her no. She said, "Then it must be your father? He is so handsome."

Again I told her no, enjoying this game quite a bit. She suggested my Uncle Paul. I said, "I love Uncle Paul but he's not handsome enough. The man I'm thinking of is the most handsome man I ever met."

Now my mother looked concerned. "Who on earth do you mean, Helga-chen?"

"Mama, do you remember that friend of yours, Herr Kreidlander? Wasn't that his name? We met him on a winter weekend getaway. To Wannasee, I think. He was by far the most handsome man ever. He gave me a present too. I would want my husband to look like him."

'My mother's face blanched at first then reddened slightly. Finally she looked amused at her own daughter's impishness. "Ach te liebe! Child! Where do you come up with these things?"

Helga laughs. 'My poor mother! That man had been one of her lovers. I don't know how many she had. My father had them too, of course. It was the way things were back then.'

I said I couldn't believe her mother had brought her along on a weekend with her lover.

'I was very young,' says Helga. 'I didn't really understand what was between them. But it was very common. Everyone had lovers.'

(Editor's note: Of course, it was the Weimar after all. Artists like Henry Miller and Egon Schiele had flourished with their shock value. Nazism abhorred art which it considered degrading to the image of Aryan purity. Jazz and blatant sexuality also seemed to stem from African origins. That didn't fit the National Socialist racial creed.)

It wasn't long before Harry suggested that Elka and Helga move into the flat with Erna. Harry himself did not live there. "You and Helga could both sleep in the attic room. It's plenty big enough."

Elka looked doubtful. "There's no need for that. We're managing fine. Though we'll need a place with heat for the winter."

"Don't give it another thought. Erna will love to have you both."

At our doorway Harry always asks my mother if she'd like to enjoy a brandy at the café on the corner. Mother always declines. Until tonight, when she accepts. She goes down after she settles me in the apartment.

"It's not that I don't love Erna," Harry would tell my mother, as they sipped their brandy at the table. "But she's just impossible sometimes. Last week I come home with flowers to surprise her with plans for dinner and dancing. She says she must polish her silver! She'd rather polish silver than go dancing! What's a man to do?"

Elka sips her brandy. "Men do what men do. I understand though. In the morning you can see your nice shiny silver." She smiles.

"You're teasing me! That's cruel!" Harry laughs.

Elka laughs too. "I have four brothers. That acquaints me with cruelty."

"How do you manage with money?" Harry was suddenly serious. "Can I help in any way?" Harry's offer came strictly from the heart, Helga would say.

"You could help me contact Berlin. If that is possible? Our Christian friend is long overdue."

"Of course, of course, my dear! I still have some business contacts there. It would be my great pleasure Frau Elka." Harry has a second brandy. "I must confess one day some time ago, Erna wouldn't let me in because the floor was wet. The landlady found me smoking a cigar on the stoop and she invited me in. How could I refuse? She's the landlady!"

Elka laughs. "You didn't! You cheated on poor Erna with her landlady? Oh God, Harry, aren't you ashamed?"

"Not really." Harry straightens up. "Like you said, men do what men do."

"Yes," says Elka. "And sometimes women do too. But we rarely brag about it."

A few minutes later, Elka says, "I must get back to Helga."

Harry says he will contact Berlin for her tomorrow.

*

'Several weeks later,' says Helga. 'A well-tailored young man arrives at our address in a taxicab. He climbs the steps outside and rings the bell.

'I opened the door for him," Helga admits. "He introduced himself and asked for my mother. He showed me a letter written in her handwriting. I showed him into the common parlor and said I would get my mother from upstairs.

'At the first landing I was challenged by the old Jewish couple who lived there.'

"Who did you let in here?" the old lady demands. "Do you know that man, child?"

"No," I say. "But he has a letter written by my mother."

"Anyone can get hold of a letter," says the old woman. "Aren't you afraid for your mother?"

"Afraid of what?"

"Nazis, of course!" shouts the old lady. "They're coming as certain as the sunrise."

The old man spoke over her. "If you'd seen what we saw in Vienna-?" Then he turns to his wife. "Poor girl! Not enough sense to be afraid!"

The old wife shakes her head. "She's not getting it, she's just not getting it."

'They were right of course,' Helga tells me. 'The old Jewish couple? I wasn't getting it. The danger! Even though we'd fled and left everything behind. I wasn't afraid of the Nazis. Somehow! It wasn't courage, Jeffrey, I wish it had been so. But it wasn't courage. Maybe the old man was right, I didn't have enough sense. It was just such a grand adventure. Our life in Berlin had been so boring! So dismal. Mother at work. Me alone with that horrid maid. Here was excitement. Everything new and different. I missed Aunt Frieda. But I loved being with mother, just the two of us all the time. I missed my father too. But I didn't think about never seeing them again. That didn't occur to me.

'The man from Berlin, a colleague of the Christian businessman in Berlin, met with my mother in the parlor of the boarding house. He also brought a letter from Erich in New York. It said, "Dearest Elka, my beloved sister, you can trust this man. He represents the best interests for you and Hans. He will ask you to sign some papers in order to keep your business going. It's better to appear to be joining them, rather than fighting. Molly was able to help our brother Martin. He is coming to us here in New York…"

"My brother says I should trust you," says Elka in a formal tone.

The young businessman smiles nervously and nods as he shuffles through the papers in his briefcase. "We want only for your husband's business to thrive, Madam. For everyone's sake. In hopes things may one day return to normal in Berlin."

The man brings out some papers from his case. He hands them to Elka to read and sign. "I have a check for you as well, Frau Wallnau. On a Swiss bank. Some modest profits we've encountered this quarter. There will be more in the future, God willing. As long as we know where to contact you."

Elka smiles at last. "Thank you. I suppose the Germans would arrest you if they knew you'd done this much."

The young man smiles back. "For the moment we are safe. With the Swiss."

Elka hands him back the signed documents. They both know she's just dissolved all legal rights to their own business enterprise. One which they'd built from nothing. One which her brother Erich had invested considerable capital. "Was there anything else?"

The young man clears his throat and seems embarrassed. "Well Frau Wallnau, my superiors have asked me to inquire about certain tailoring designs that you may have brought with you. It seems there was a design for a three-piece men's ensemble. It was unique in terms of style and cut, we understand. These changes making it much more affordable."

"You haven't found them in our offices?" says Elka.

"Not as yet, ma'am."

"I shall write to my husband and ask him about the designs."

The young man stands up. He looks very uncomfortable. "Frau Wallnau, please understand, you should know no one feels good about any of this." He tries to put a smile on his face. "Maybe it blows over before too long? After all, who in Germany doesn't have some Jewish in the bloodline?"

Elka simply nods her head and sighs. The young man thanks her, shakes her hand and then takes his leave.

Only a few minutes later my mother, Elka sat inside our tiny apartment with those exact tailoring designs on her lap. She was looking through them idly along with the letter from Erich. "I remember the night we showed these designs to your Uncle Erich. Your father and I, we were so proud," mother tells me. "We wanted to bring him in as an investor. You understand?"

"Oh yes, mother. The same night Father insulted your Aunt Molly? After she'd served her lovely dinner and all. Little morsels, barely a bite or two. And then Father asks, 'So, Molly? When do we eat?'"

My mother laughs. "Molly never forgave him. Who told you that story?"

"Aunt Frieda. She said Aunt Molly still complained about how long it took the Nazis to process Erich's divorce papers from his first wife."

Elka laughs again, but her laughter is tinged with melancholy.

"Oh mama! That's the best part of all of this!"

"What's that Liebchen?"

"That I don't have to go play with Cousin Marion!"

"Oh dear Lord!" Elka sighs and reaches out to hug Helga. "Liebchen-liebchen! Come, let me show you about these designs…"

Chapter Five

The Terror Arrives

'On a bright clear day in May of 1940' Helga recalls. 'My mother had come by the lovely school to pick me up. We were walking home when we bumped into Erna and she joined us. Just at that moment a squadron of fighter planes roared above our heads.'

Erna says, "They must be doing maneuvers." She quickens her step. "Come! We can watch them from my place."

Once we are installed out on Erna's balcony another squadron of planes flies over. Helga says, "I told them those planes are German."

"They can't be, child!" Erna counters, just as we hear some explosions and see plumes of black smoke start to rise in the distance.

"God in heaven, they're here!" my mother murmurs.

"The Germans?" cries Erna. "No, Elka! It's not possible! It's too soon!"

More explosions follow and they sound closer.

"Come inside," my mother says. "Erna, we must hear what the radio has to say." And we all three scurry inside moving off the balcony.

'The planes bombed Brussels haphazardly, here and there, for about a week,' Helga recalls. 'Then a week or so after that the tanks and trucks rolled through. In their wake they left hundreds of young German boys. Nazis of course. But somehow I didn't see them that way. I saw them as Germans, like me. School stopped. They declared early summer holidays. Even though everyone seemed frightened out of their wits, I was secretly glad to have gotten out of exams.'

(Editor's note: Six months after that the streets of Brussels are decorated with giant red and black swastika flags. Nazi soldiers are a common sight on the sidewalks. However, the Nazis treat Belgium differently from occupied Holland and France. In Belgium they leave local police and politicians in place. Most all local governments are left undisturbed and for the first two years of the occupation, Belgian resistance is mild. A group of prominent Jewish men act as liaison between the occupier Nazis and the greater Jewish community. Not until the Nazi imposition of the mandatory yellow Stars of David to be worn by Jews in public, does the Belgian resistance really kick into high gear. They begin bombing train tracks and depots. And in fact Yellow Stars were worn by many non-Jews among the general Belgian population as a snub to the occupiers.)

Helga says, 'At this time my mother still receives the occasional letter from my father in the Dutch internment camp. But now the camp is under Nazi control.'

Clutching a new letter from Hans, Elka dashes into the café where she is greeted by the familiar bartender. It is fall and Helga is back in school with the nuns. The waiter brings Elka a small pot of coffee. When she thanks him, he nods towards a table in the corner where four Nazi officers are enjoying a bottle of schnapps. Elka sips her coffee and fingers her letter nervously. Now and then she glances over at the table with the soldiers. She wears the same fur coat, now cleaned and repaired, which got her across the border a year and a half ago. The Nazis are loud.

"To Belgium!" says one raising his glass. "A great addition to the Reich!"

A second officer lifts his glass. "Yah! Good food and soft women!"

The first officer shouts at the bartender. "Another bottle here, sir! And a drink for you too! We like your country, Belge!"

"Yes!" shouts a third Nazi. "In six months we've improved things for everyone. Increased overtime pay. And free medical benefits!"

When the bartender brings them a fresh bottle, the first Nazi says, "So, monsieur, how do you find life under National Socialism?"

The bartender shrugs. "Since you boys arrived, my business is off by half."

"Maybe he prefers to be a serf under feudal king Leopold?" says one Nazi.

"Well," says the first Nazi. "If he's so depressed, he can get free medical treatment for his condition." And all four Nazis roar with laughter.

Elka hears another Nazi say in German slang, "These Belge are too stupid to know when they're better off."

She picks up the letter from Hans and opens it. The first part tells how the Dutch camp has now been taken over by the Nazis. No one will be allowed to emigrate freely. He tells of his grave concern for her and Helga and how they should be receiving money from the man in Berlin. "…Enclosed you will find a poem I managed to compose. It is the only thing I can offer you in the way of a gift, Elka, my love, my darling wife. I never imagined how much I could love you and Helga until this separation." As she reads, the bartender sets a small glass of brandy beside her. They exchange smiles.

Above: Hans Wallnau 1925
Helga's father

Elka reads the poem from Hans. "You captured my heart darling Elka/ When as a child, you smiled, so shyly/ A smile like sparkling pearls/ When you sang with a voice like a summer's nightingale/ And your eyes shone as brightly as shooting stars in the sky/ When older we grew and you allowed me to court you/ Never did I dare think I'd surpass your legion of admirers/ With their wealth and wit and glittering style…" Elka's tears are streaming freely down her cheeks and she pauses to wipe them away.

The Nazis can still be heard talking too loudly in the corner. "They will come to love the Third Reich just as we do!" one of them bellows. "They will see what a Jew-free society can be!"

Elka continues reading her letter. "When you accepted the flame in my heart, my love/ You ignited a passion in my soul/ Kissing your lips was like floating on rose petals/ Touching your skin was like the downy silk of warm snowflakes in Wannsee/ Making love was like drifting up into heavenly splendor/ A wonderland of blissful sensations/ Like those known only to devotees of the lotus blossom/ Feeling your love in return was like being swaddled in soft delight/ Like being flooded from within by a bubbly warm spring/ Your love spread fire through my limbs/ Made my head swim as though filled with champagne/ My darling heart!/ My precious soul!/ How wonderful are my dreams when you are here with me/ Your laughter fills my heart with unspeakable joy…"

It was at that moment Erna burst into the café. She looked frantic and panicked. She rushes up to Elka. "They've taken Harry! My Harry! The Gestapo! They found him carrying American money. A Jew! Elka, they've arrested him! Oh my poor Harry!"

"Oh dear God!" says Elka. "Sit down. Have a sip of brandy." She glances over at the table of Nazis. Erna follows her glance.

"No! I need a whiskey," says Erna and she signals the bartender. Erna notices the letter. "Something from Hans?"

Elka nods. "A poem. I never knew he could write anything like this."

The bartender brings Erna a whiskey and he nods subtly in the direction of the Nazis. "Are you all right?" he asks softly. "What's happened?"

Erna tells him the news about Harry.

The bartender shakes his head. "What was he doing with American money?"

"It was a show of faith," Erna answers. "To get him out. They insisted it be American dollars."

"Damn! Was it a trap then?"

Erna shrugs. "No. I don't know. Maybe it was?"

The bartender nods his head and leaves. Elka fingers her letter, then folds it and puts it in her purse. She and Erna commiserate for a while. Finally Elka says she must collect Helga from school. She invites Erna to their apartment for some dinner.

At first Erna says, "Oh no! I must be there in case there's word about Harry."

But Elka persuades her she should eat something to help calm down.

'To our surprise,' says Helga. 'When we all three arrive home, we find cousin Bernie waiting for us. Elka makes the introductions. Erna tells Bernie about Harry right away.

Bernie says, "If he has money, it will help. If he has enough money, he can buy his way out. That's what I know."

Erna looks relieved. "Oh God, I pray you're right."

A short time later we are all eating soup, liverwurst and rye bread. For Erna's sake Bernie retells how he got to Brussels. "We both had exit visas, my father and I," he says. "The Nazis didn't care. My father answered his police summons. He never believed people could do this. The Nazis threw him in jail. When I went to the police station to show them the visas, they took them away from me and arrested me too. I was put on the same train as my father, but in a different car. They made us change trains in the middle of the night. Everyone was saying it was the train to the death camp. As they herded us onto the new train, I saw a chance to escape into the woods and I took it. There was no chance to help father."

"Oh! Poor Josi!" cries Elka. "He was the sweetest of all of us! So quiet all the time. Like a little mouse."

"How did you get across the border?" Erna asks Bernie.

"I walked," he says. "Two days through the forest of the Ardennes. I followed the river. Finally I got a lift on a farmer's wagon to a town near Dinant. Some resistance people helped me from there."

"Nazi devil bastards!" says Erna. "We've got them crawling up our ass here too now."

"Brussels is not so bad," Bernie counters. "You still have your own police and mayor. And no general round-ups yet.

"I'm getting out of Belgium. With my Harry! Oh God!" Erna looks stricken as she recalls the situation. "I must help him get free. I must speak with some people." She barely touches her food.

*

'Money got scarce after Harry's arrest,' Helga recalls. 'Aunt' Erna still seemed to have enough. But my mother Elka had less and less. Very little came from Berlin. Though every few months the young businessman Rosenfeld, a Christian, would show up, sometimes with his timid wife. She looked so much like him she might've been his twin. They both spoke of hope. But they both looked afraid.

Cousin Bernie came over to Erna's flat on Christmas for dinner.

My mother and I had just recently moved into Erna's attic bedroom. With Harry gone, she felt better having company with her now. Harry had always had his own place, but he'd spent many nights there.

"I went to the police to try to find out about him," Erna says. "They wouldn't tell me a thing. Nothing! They treated me like a criminal just for asking about him." Her face turns fearful. "I don't believe I'll ever see him again!"

"Oh Erna!" cries Elka. "Don't say that! Please! I still believe Hans and I will be together again. This Nazi madness will have to end sooner or later."

"Harry said it's too late already." Erna pauses. "I've seen enough, I'm getting out!"

"Have you found someone to help you?" asks Elka. "Someone you can trust?"

"No. But I have some feelers out. Something will come through for me."

Silence fell over the table for a moment. We all knew it was different for Erna. She was a Christian. Her Harry had been a Jew.

"We may be all right here," says Bernie out of the blue. "Belgians are different. With their passive resistance."

"God help us!" cries Elka. "I really don't understand any of it. Did Germany declare war on Europe? Or just on Jews?"

"Both, Aunt Elka!" says Bernie. "Hitler wants a Yid-free Europe."

"But three-quarters of all Germans have some Jewish blood. For godsakes, Hitler himself!"

Bernie nods with a wry smile. "Yes, yes. But who will admit it? We are vermin, you know? Besides if you know the right people, you buy yourself papers that make you Gentile. Very simple."

'After dinner,' Helga recalls, 'I sat with Bernie in the living room near Erna's small Christmas tree. Bernie asks me about the plans to send me to Zurich to live with my Uncle Paul. I tell him about Uncle Paul's fiancée and her attempted suicide.'

"It would've been very different for me," Helga tells Bernie. "I would've become a singer I have no doubt!"

Bernie nods. "No doubt. They were very rich, this family?"

"Oh yes! They owned the biggest theater in Zurich. I could've had a career!"

"You mean you have no interest in the clothing business?" Bernie asks and Helga shakes her head no. Then Bernie says, "I've been meaning to ask if your father's business is still operating?"

"As far as we know," I tell him. "But we've heard nothing in some time now."

"Did they ever go ahead with the plans for the three-piece suit? The affordable ensemble?"

"You know about that?" Helga says surprised. "The design of my father's?"

"Yes, I knew about it. My father admired it too, you know? Said it was a money-maker."

"Well I know nothing about it. As I said, we've heard nothing from Berlin in some time now."

"I'm sorry," says Bernie. 'And I'm sorry for your father." He pauses. "I've found some freelance tailoring work."

"That's good," says Helga. "It'll help keep you going." She hesitates. "Just watch out you don't go tailoring for the Nazis." As soon as I say it, I see my cousin turn red. That meant he probably was tailoring Nazi uniforms already. After all the Belgians weren't going to do it.

*

'The thing was,' Helga recalls. 'I still hadn't started hating the Nazis yet. Not in my heart. Even as terrible as they were. It wasn't until my poor mother was forced to sell her beautiful fur coat. Oh! How we both loved that coat! It wasn't fair mother had to sell it. Almost like surrendering the family colors. But then food had become suddenly so expensive. We lived with Erna. But we didn't expect her to support us too.

'It was now spring of 1942. We'd left Berlin three years ago.

'Mother told me she wouldn't need a big fur coat in the summer and she'd find a new coat in the fall. I cried. And I began to hate the Nazis. I had a growth spurt around that time and I started to look older than I was. More than once some men in the café would try to buy us drinks, my mother and me. Actually try to pick us up!

'Mother still loved to hang out in the café. She even sang on occasion. My mother had a beautiful voice too. People would beg her to sing.

'It was around that time she started to make me eat dinner at the house of these other friends of hers. A Christian couple, the Dorfs, that was their name. They had piles of money. Mr. Dorf was thin and handsome, like Frank Sinatra. The wife was as fat as a house!' Helga laughs. 'The food was very fine. But I still hated going over there. The daughter had nothing to say, she just sat there, neither black nor white.' Helga laughs again. 'My mother was friends with Mr. Dorf's mistress also. Dorf didn't have his woman on the side, as you say. He had her right there on his plate in front of him. Along with his wife!

'Aunt' Erna meanwhile kept trying to make a contact to help her get out of Belgium. Everyone knew someone, who knew someone, connected to the Resistance or the Underground. Erna would speak to people in the café. It was dangerous. I wondered often at the risk she took.

'Even stranger was how many nights all through the wee small hours, Erna would sit hunched over the upholstery on a genuine Victorian wingback loveseat. She patiently undid the stitching one thread at a time. Once she'd opened up a small section she would sew individual gold coins which Harry had left her into the backing of the loveseat. One by one! One coin at a time. She sewed them in there tight, then she stitched it all back up again. All neat as a pin! I'd spied her one night on a late trip to the bathroom. I'd never told anyone. Not even my mother.

Chapter Six

Hiding Jews in the Attic

'One morning just after dawn there came a sharp knock on the door. Crack! Erna opens it to see two Nazis standing there. One is an officer, a captain with white gloves and ridiculously shiny boots. The other is a corporal in a drab green trench coat and a helmet. He is taller and thicker than the captain with his flashy uniform.'

"We have orders to search this house!" the Captain barks. The Corporal snaps his heels together.

Erna smiles broadly. "Fine! I have nothing to hide. You're welcome to see for yourself." And she swings the door wide open.

The Captain and Corporal enter the flat. The Captain smooths his gloved hands. "We have information that you are hiding gold coins, Fraulein Unghar!"

Erna laughs loudly. "Gold? Would I still be here in Brussels with gold? I would be gone long ago, if I had gold!" She looks back and forth between the two. "How ridiculous!"

"I don't know about that, Fraulein. But we will ascertain the truth soon enough."

'We heard them enter and begin a methodical search of each room. Slowly and carefully they opened every drawer, every cupboard, sideboard and armoire. They poked and prodded and moved everything around. They emptied everything out and threw it everywhere, while Erna scurried around behind them putting things back in order.

'My mother and I can hear them moving from room to room below us. Systematically they search, though the Captain does very little of the actual work. The Captain is careful not to soil his pristine white gloves or his shining uniform. He directs the poor Corporal around pointing out this object or that for the Corporal to ransack. Meanwhile every moment the Captain watches Erna's face, in case her expression might reveal the hiding place.

'These Nazis believe utterly and completely in the moral correctness of their actions. Their search is extremely precise. Even so, after several hours of finding nothing, it appears as if the Corporal at least is losing patience. As each room comes up empty Erna adopts a stronger air of vindication. The Captain remains obstinate.

"What are they doing, mama?" I ask my mother.

"They are searching. Everything and everywhere," she tells me.

"Are they searching for us?"

"No, darling. I don't think so. Stay in your bed."

'On and on it went until finally they climb the stairs to our attic bedroom. My mother and I are still in our beds. One on each side of the room. The two Nazis push the attic door open and come right in. My mother just sits there. She wore a dressing gown over her nightclothes. She merely looked at them.

'My bed was a sleeping couch and I lay there with a thick blanket over my bad leg. I'd had several operations lately and it was still in a big plaster cast. Erna comes in behind the Nazis.'

"Well now," the Captain turns to Erna. His gaze sweeps over the flowered wallpaper and takes in both my mother and me. "It would seem every house in Brussels is hiding Jews in the attic."

The Corporal snickers at that and the Captain approaches Helga's bed.

"What's the matter with this one?" the Captain chides. "You lazy, girl? Don't want to get out of bed?" He turns to the Corporal. "Search the bedding!"

The Corporal throws back the covers. "Look! Captain! Her leg is in a cast!"

"I can see that!" the Captain snaps. "Check underneath her!" And the Captain proceeds to brush invisible dust off his uniform. He checks his white gloves for dirt or lint. "Then search her mother's bed as well."

The Captain checks his gloves and uniform compulsively, while at the same time he keeps a sly watch on Erna in the mirror. He watches her face intently for the slightest trace of fear or apprehension.

'The Corporal seems embarrassed as he pushes his fingers deep into my bedding, poking his hands in all under and around me. He turns to the Captain and raises empty hands. The Captain then directs him all over the room telling him to look in here or in there. Open-up this or that! All the while the Captain keeps focused on Erna's face for a telltale giveaway. Erna's face shows nothing.

'As he searches Mama's bedding, I realize for the first time the velvet loveseat has been moved up here into our bedroom. I hadn't noticed before. I drew a sharp breath at the sight of it. The Corporal moved from my mother's bed to the loveseat. He pushes and prods at the velvet upholstery but nothing seems out of order. There is only the sound of old springs. Erna remains stone-faced. My mother's face is also a study in composure. Underneath I know she is both horrified and deeply embarrassed that German men like this can soak up all the Nazi blather. How average Germans can behave like this in a foreign country?'

"So, Fraulein Unghar! It would appear you want to send us away empty-handed?" the Captain addresses Erna. His manner is all puffed up. "Unless maybe we take these two Jews with us? Maybe they have swallowed up your gold dollars, Frau Unghar?"

"I have no gold dollars or gold anything! As your search has revealed." Erna sounds very firm and solid. "There is no gold in this house."

The Captain puffed out his chest. "Maybe we take them anyway." The Captain smiles. "Arresting Jews is always good business! Corporal!"

"Forget it, Captain," the Corporal says abruptly and almost insolently. "There is nothing in my orders about carrying a girl in a cast down those treacherous stairs." Everyone is surprised. The remark breaks the tension, like a crack in the glass. It was funny, but no one laughs.

"Ach Corporal! You are no fun at all!" And at that the Captain claps his gloved-hands together, still lily-white. "All right! Let's get out of here, Corporal. It is almost time for lunch." As he passes Erna, he eyes her closely. "Remember Frau Unghar! Possession of American gold money is a capital crime. It carries an automatic death sentence."

Erna stares back at him unblinking. "I have no gold money. As you've seen, Captain."

"None that we found today." The Captain leans in closer. "But it is possible, we will come back and look again."

"Come back anytime you like," Erna sounds as defiant as ever.

'Erna follows them out and down, and watches through the window as they leave. After that Erna returns to the attic with a bottle of brandy and three glasses. Her eyes twinkle mischief, as her hand caresses the loveseat.

*

'That was the summer I turned sixteen. During August the weather in Brussels was beautiful. My friend Ruthie and I loved to go to the municipal swimming pool every chance we could. Ruthie had been a schoolmate of mine in Berlin as well and I'd met her accidently at the lovely Catholic school here in Brussels. Half-Christian, Ruthie was the friend I was with the night of the movie, when I was questioned by the Gestapo soldier. But that happened sometime later.

'This day the municipal pool was crowded. Sometimes we would just sit on the edge and dangle our legs in the water. This afternoon we found ourselves falling under the attentions of two strapping young German boys just slightly older than we were. The boys were so surprised to hear us speak German. They began to tease us and flirt back and forth. They traded some jokes and splashed around pleasantly. When it came time for the pool to close the boys asked if we would meet them outside and go for coffee at the café nearby. We said yes. Without thinking.

'Ruthie and I were both very excited and nervous to wait for these boys. We'd never seen them before and they seemed so charming. Oddly enough we were changed and dressed before them. Ruthie and I are outside the pool waiting and we laugh and poke each other in good fun.

'Then all at once I notice the two boys approaching. They are now dressed in their shiny gray Nazi uniforms.'

"Oh my God!" Helga exclaims to me. She suddenly stops laughing. "How stupid of us not to realize!"

Then she continues, 'Ruthie could only stand there shaking her head.

'These two boys were absolutely thrilled that we had waited for them. They escort us across the street to the café. Over our coffee drinks, one soldier speaks to me and the other speaks to Ruthie. They must have decided between themselves. The one with me was named Heinz and he tells me he thinks I'm very cute. I wonder right away if they think we are like some girls we know? Girls who would go off into the woods with Nazi soldiers. They traded favors for food coupons. Off to the woods they'd go and when they came back their pockets were stuffed. Ruthie and I were not like those girls.'

"Thank you," I tell Heinz smiling faintly. "You are very handsome yourself."

"I don't mean to flatter you," says Heinz. "Not in any false way. I mean that you look to me as if you belong to a very special club."

"What club is that?" I ask having no idea what he's going to say.

"Why, 'The-Never-Been-Kissed Club' of course."

Helga laughs. "Why on earth would you think that?"

Heinz grins charmingly. "A look in the eye. I can always tell."

Eye Contact   47

"Well," Helga laughs again. "You're completely wrong about me. I'm a bad girl, really. I know all sorts of terrible naughty things."

"Really? Like what?"

"Oh! I never tell!"

'After the coffee the boys offer to escort us across the park over to the trolley stand. We hold hands, both of us, Ruthie and I with our Nazi soldiers, as we cross the grass. My soldier Heinz he holds my hand and then he stops to kiss me. A chaste kiss, lightly on the lips. Maybe to see how I would react? Of course, he was right. I was a member of that club. Even though I'd done some naughty things with a cousin of mine years and years before. This was my first romantic kiss. I knew about a lot of things which I'd never actually done.

'I knew girls who went off into the woods with soldiers like these. Girls who did things with Nazi soldiers. For food coupons. I didn't blame them. I didn't judge them. Everyone was hungry all the time now. I just couldn't imagine doing it myself. But I enjoyed my first real kiss with my Nazi soldier friend. Heinz was handsome and funny and I knew I would never see him again. Even though I would've loved to. I couldn't exactly bring him home or even tell my mother. When we parted that evening we told them we'd look for them again. And in fact we did. But we never saw either of them again.

*

'One night around that time we were still living with Erna, she was late coming home. My mother started to get nervous.

"I can't believe Erna's not home yet. It's almost dark outside. Isn't she always home by now?"

"Yes," I nod my head. "But it doesn't mean-"

"No, I know, I know! I just worry, that's all."

'A short time later there's a knock at the door and I go to answer. It's my cousin Bernie. He's flushed and out of breath as if he'd run the whole way. He tells us Erna has been arrested. She's being held by the Gestapo.'

"How do you know this?" my mother asks.

Bernie says, "One of my tailoring clients, he works close to the Gestapo. They're still convinced your friend has American gold dollars."

I say, "But they searched this house from top to bottom."

"Maybe because of Harry?" says my mother.

"When I heard her name," says Bernie. "I thought I'd better come over to warn you, Aunt Elka. You and Helga. Maybe I could help you find a new place?"

I look to my mother. "We are still safe here aren't we mama?"

"Yes, darling, I think so. If they'd wanted us I think they would've come back."

We were both remembering the Nazi Captain his white gloves and his cruel humor.

"They know we're here," mother adds.

'We were terrified for Erna of course. But there was nothing to do but carry on. Wait and hope. Life wasn't normal. But normal things still happened. Mother and I are eating one day in the café and being tended to by the familiar bartender. He arrives carrying two small snifters of brandy.'

He says, "The two gentlemen over there insisted I bring you these with their compliments."

"Oh!" I let out a little shriek.

The bartender chuckles, "I know, Frau Elka, but I thought, why spoil their fun?" He nods towards the gents. "Not that it would bother the likes of those two."

Elka smiles indulgently. "Please thank them, Francois. But no thank you."

I was disappointed. "Oh mama!"

The bartender picked up the snifters. "Any news of Erna?" he asks. My mother shakes her head no. He then carries the drinks back over to the two gentlemen. He tells them something, they laugh somewhat embarrassed. They look over and raise their drinks in friendly salute.

'The next day I was alone at Erna's when my cousin Bernie shows up. I invite him in for a cup of tea. He asks about my mother. She is at a doctor's appointment.'

"Is there anything wrong?" he asks.

"I don't know. Mother won't tell me. She doesn't want me to worry." I look at Bernie. "Do you have any news of Erna?"

Bernie shakes his head. "No. Are you going to take my coat, cousin?"

"Take it yourself, cousin. I will make us tea. What do you think they will do to Erna?"

"Nothing much. Because she is a Christian. They will probably let her go." Bernie takes a thin package out and drops it on the table. It's wrapped in butcher paper.

"What's that?"

Bernie smiles. "Sliced ham."

"Oh! How wonderful! I can't even remember the last time." I continue fixing the tea.

A few minutes later we are enjoying tea together. Then Bernie tells me, "It's going to get tougher for us here, cousin. The Nazis want all Jews to start wearing yellow stars on the outside of our clothing."

"Yellow stars?" I say.

"The Star of David. The Jewish star. Symbol of the faith."

"Who's faith?"

Bernie laughs. "Our faith! The Jewish faith! Sweet cousin, do you even know that you're Jewish?"

"Don't anger me!" I tell him. "Or you can take your lovely ham and scram!"

"Okay, okay, I'm just teasing you cousin."

"Well," I tell him. "The truth is I don't know anything about being Jewish."

Bernie shrugs. "Who did? Before all this."

"Would you hear if something happens to Erna?"

"Maybe," he says. "Or maybe not." Bernie shifts uneasily. "I'll ask some of my contacts."

I realize then, Bernie must be tailoring for the Nazis. Everyone survives however they can. I don't judge him. But it must be dangerous too.

Bernie leans in closer to me. "What I'm wondering about are those suit patterns? The three-piece ensemble that your father designed. Do you know what I mean? I might have found the right people here in Brussels."

"I have no idea what you're talking about," I tell him. "Besides those are my father's designs. For when Papa comes back and we return to Berlin."

"Yes, of course. I understand. Uncle Hans is coming back. This could be a help to him then?"

"I told you I don't know what happened to the patterns."

'We hear the front door open and my mother comes in. She looks weary. She greets Bernie, who mentions bringing the ham. Mother thanks him and insists he stay and have some with them.'

"No, Auntie," says Bernie. "I brought it for you and Helga."

'That's when I begin to realize my mother is not feeling well at all. We lay there up in our attic bedroom and I could hear her breathing. It was troubled. She sounded worried now, even in her sleep. The little Victorian loveseat sat there still. Unmolested. How much money did Erna have sewn up in the backing? God only knows!

'On the third night since Erna'd been arrested my mother and I were eating a meagre dinner when we heard the key turn in the latch. We turned to see Erna standing there. She looked fine and quite delighted.

'We all three shriek with joy. My mother stands up to embrace her friend.'

"Erna! Darling! You're home!" They hug each other a moment. Then Erna steps back and does a few quick dance steps. She taps her feet and flutters her hands.

"They had to let me go!" Erna cries. "They have nothing on me!"

'Then she disappears for a brief moment. I hear her climb the stairs. To check the loveseat, no doubt. When she returns she carries a bottle of port wine.'

"I was locked up with the absolute dregs of Brussels!" Erna tells us proudly, as she retrieves three small glasses from the cupboard. "Cheap grotesque old prostitutes and mean hard drunks. The worst women you can possibly imagine. Just when I got used to one cell, they'd move me into another. They interrogated me night and day about Harry's money. And where it was! Where had he gotten his American dollars? They kept telling me I wouldn't be released until I told them everything. And especially where I was hiding the rest of Harry's money."

She laughs and pours us all some port.

"So I kept telling them they'd be supporting me for the rest of the war because I had no gold, no money hidden anywhere. They starved me for two days. They disrupted my sleep. They threatened me. I just stuck to my story and told them I didn't care how long they kept me locked up."

My mother laughs and raises her glass in a toast. "Perfect! To your release!" We all clinked glasses and Erna laughs.

"Yes, yes! They got so sick of hearing me, they let me go!" says Erna.

We are all happy to be together again. "But Aunt Erna?" I ask. "Why did they arrest you after they searched here and all?"

Erna shrugs. "I don't know. Maybe I spoke to the wrong people in the café? About getting out. But I'm still going. I can't stay here with all this anymore. I'm sorry for you both, but I can't. Now I hear they've started up with the yellow stars. I have to be more careful about my contacts. They're watching me still."

"Weren't you scared out of your wits?" I ask.

"Of those Nazi creeps? I wouldn't give them the satisfaction, Helga dear."

'Erna was Christian. She wouldn't be forced to wear a star. But it was all too much for her. Losing her Harry had hit her hard. The Resistance had given her the news. Harry ended up in a camp in France. He'd been in such bad shape he'd tried to kill himself. But he'd survived and was still alive.

'Erna was amazing! For a Gentile, she had real chutzpah. Two days after she was released, she returned to the police station. When they asked what she wanted, she told them. "I want to compliment you on what a thorough job you've done in determining my innocence."

She was still laughing that evening when she told us. "I marched right up to that captain and said, 'I want to thank you for doing such an excellent job! It really proves you know what you're doing'."

'We all three laugh again.'

My mother says, "You're lucky they didn't take offense and slap you back in a cell."

"I know, I know!" says Erna gleefully. "But I just couldn't resist. It was silly, but I couldn't help myself."

Chapter Seven

Belgium Gets the Yellow Stars/ Mama's Operation

(Editor's note: Belgium was the last of the Nazi occupied countries to require Jews to wear the six-sided Star of David in yellow, visible on their clothing any time they were out in public. This was in the spring of 1942. All Belgians became incensed at this imposition and immediately non-Jews began sewing stars on their clothing in solidarity with their Jewish countrymen. Also around this time the Belgian resistance, relatively low-key, stepped up their activities dramatically. They began bombing trains in the countryside and seriously disrupted German rail transport.)

Helga recalls, 'I remember finding my mother sewing the hideous yellow star on the outside of my favorite coat.'

"Oh God, mama! No! Not on my good coat, please! That star is so terribly ugly! Please don't!"

"Helga darling, we have no choice. If you don't wear the star, they can arrest you." Mother continues to push the needle and thread through the heavy material, a silver thimble protects the tip of her finger.

"Oh mama!" I cried. "It's so ugly!"

"I know Liebchen, I know. But I want you to have dinner with the Dorf's tonight. I'm worried you're not getting enough to eat. And my friend, Mrs. Dorf, she says they miss you coming over."

"No!" Helga stamps her foot. "I'd rather starve, mama! I can't go over there anymore. It's too strange!"

My mother heaves a sigh. "All right, all right, Helga-chen." Mother looks tired and pale.

"Maybe it's time for Uncle Walter's curse."

"What on earth are you talking about?"

"Don't you remember? Did I never tell you?" I laugh. Mother smiles curiously at me. "At the big dinner at Uncle Erich's and Aunt Molly's, when I took the last sweet potato from the serving platter. The one Uncle Walter wanted. He looked at me and said, 'You should know what it's like to be hungry someday'."

"Oh dear!" Mother shakes her head. "Poor Walter. He was always the most serious. Did you know there was a story of Walter, from when your father and them were all growing up? The maid stepped on a needle and it went right into her foot. When Walter tried to pull it out, he only got the thread. She had to go to the hospital." I knew the story. It made us both laugh. "God only knows what's happened to him. And dear Frieda."

Above: Walter Wallnau 1925
(Helga's uncle)

*

'So I wore the coat with the star. But I had this very large handbag, which I carried high up on my shoulder. It concealed the star nicely. As I said, nothing was normal. Yet normal things still happened. We went to the movie theater whenever we could. I often went with Ruthie who was only half-Jewish. But she still had to wear the star.

'The night I had the encounter with the Gestapo, Ruthie was nervous for me. When we came out of the theater, it was already a quarter to eight. Curfew was eight o'clock.'

"Isn't it strange, Ruthie! How they make Jews wear this star, which makes us seem special. But they hate Jews for thinking they're special. Is that it? They call themselves Chosen People and all? Does any of it make sense?"

Ruthie shakes her head no. "I wear my top coat over the star." She looks at Helga. "I'm not supposed to, I know but it's cold tonight."

"You need a handbag like mine."

"None of this makes sense, Helga. And it's late now, look! You better come with me to our house tonight."

"No, no, I can make it! My mother would worry herself sick."

'Ruthie protests a little more, but finally we hug and part ways. She lives in the opposite direction. I watch Ruthie a moment, then I adjust the handbag on my shoulder. That's when the man in the long black coat comes up and speaks to me. His coat was leather. He spoke in German. We were just a few feet from the theater.

(Editor's note: Helga related this same incident several times over the course of our interviews. We present it again here in its proper chronological place for purposes of clarity.)

'He was handsome and not that far from me in age. Just a few years. He had fair hair and light blue eyes. He looks rather sweet to me and his accent tells me he is Ausland Deutsche, from the German countryside. However I am also aware he is with the Gestapo, the central Nazi office.

"Guttentag, young Fraulein! Did you enjoy the picture show tonight?" He addresses me in a polite German tone.

"Yes, thank you, sir," I reply in kind.

His voice changes. "Ya, I knew it! You're a German Jew! Where is your star?"

I shift the handbag on my shoulder and reveal the dingy yellow cloth star.

"Why do you hide it like this? It is forbidden to conceal the star! Do you know this?"

I stand up straight and look this young Nazi right in the eye. "I wear my handbag over it. Because it is so ugly on my nice coat." Still holding his eye I say to him. "What would you do if they made you wear an ugly old thing on your nice leather coat?"

The merest trace of humor flashes momentarily in the Gestapo's blue eyes. "Let me see your identity card. You know I could arrest you just for this?"

I fished around in the handbag and found it. The Nazi studied the card for a moment. Then he says, "You live at this address here?" I nod yes. "Well you can't possibly make it back there before the curfew."

"Yes, I believe I can. I'm not late yet."

"But you will be late. This address is almost two kilometers away. And I see you don't walk that well."

I held eye contact with him. "I'd be a third of the way there by now, if you hadn't stopped me."

"Young woman! I could shoot you now and my superiors would give me a medal for it. Do you realize that?"

"Really? Your superiors have something to fear from a young girl such as me?"

"What!" The Gestapo laughs sharply. "You're quite something, aren't you!" His eyes show no humor. "But you are a Jew. With your star hidden. In violation of curfew. If I arrest you, I would get a commendation at the very least."

"How nice for you."

His eyes drill me. I stare back. He says, "It would look good on my record."

"I'm sure it would. Is that what you're going to do?"

"Can you give me one reason why I should not?"

"Only one," I say. "It would kill my dear mother."

"Your Jewish mother? What could she possibly matter to me? I should kill you both!"

I said nothing now. I simply held eye contact with him. It felt as if I had to do so.

"Fraulein? Do you have any idea what it means to be Jewish?"

I shook my head. "No," I say. And I merely look back at him. My face showed neither hatred nor fear. It was a test of wills, I understood. He held my gaze.

"Were you bat mitzvah'd?"

"No."

"Do you speak Hebrew?" And he recites a quick Hebrew prayer.

"No."

"Do you speak Jewish?" By which he means Yiddish.

"No."

He looks at me for a long while, then he says, "Isn't it sad you should die for something you know nothing about?"

It was a question we both thought about for a moment. What was the point of killing people who understood nothing? "You are going to kill me then?"

"Yes! The very next time I catch out this close to curfew." He hands me back my identity card. "And do not conceal your star. Get going now!" He watches as I scurry off.

Helga says, 'I didn't even thank him or anything, I thought later on. But thank him for what? For not being the mindless unthinking Nazi he was trained to be? Was I afraid at that moment? Everyone always asks that. There were worse moments, so it is hard to say. I suppose I was afraid, but more for my mother, I think.

'Of course I must've been afraid on one level,' Helga tells me. 'But my instincts told me not to show it. That to show my fear would be fatal. It would arouse fear in him! And if his fear wins him over, it would be a gamble for me. I didn't dare tell my mother about the incident. It would've worried her to death. And she wasn't even well herself. Though she refused to tell me what was the matter. She was pale oftentimes and weak.

'Erna was gone by now. She'd made her contact and that was that. She left. She helped us out with a little money before she left.

'Mother and I found a furnished room in a large house with lots of tenants. The landlady was a giant fat Frenchwoman, who went around screaming for her niece, "Betsy! Betsy!"'

Helga laughs.

'Betsy was her slave. Betsy did all the cleaning and mopping. I met some wonderful people in that building. Jews from all over. All in hiding. Very well educated. Lawyers and the like. I have to wonder if any of them survived? I remember one in particular. An old Jewish man, he said to me, "It worries me that you show no fear, child. Your fear is not in the right place."

'I didn't understand him then. But they were nice people, I liked them.

*

'I was in and out of the hospital all the time myself that spring. I had two or three operations to fix my leg. Then in May my mother and I went into the hospital at the same time. We were both scheduled for surgery in the same week, mine was considered minor.

'We were about the same height, mother and I, and we entered the hospital arm in arm.'

"Mother?" I say in surprise. "Where is your star? You never sewed it on?"

"No," she answers absently. "I must get around to doing that soon."

"You could be arrested!"

My mother smiles. "Not here in the hospital."

"Oh mama!" I shiver from a sudden chill. "Must they operate on you? Is there no other way?"

"I explained it to you, Liebchen. Just as they explained it to me. It's the thyroid gland. Here in my neck." She touches the spot. "Given what is, surgery is the best solution. We are still Jews, Helga darling. We cannot move about freely anymore. If they operate now, I stand the best chance to recover in the shortest time."

'Later that same day I was standing beside my mother's bed in the hospital.'

"Mama! You must change your doctor! Don't let this man operate on you, please! His last two patients died on the surgical table. Mama, please!"

She looks at me and smiles. "It's okay, darling! If the last two died, that means the chances for me are good."

"No mama! All his patients die!" I hug her. She is in her hospital gown and there are bandages around her neck. "It's okay," she says to me. "You must have your consultation with the doctor. I'll be right here when you come back."

Below: Elka Oling Wallnau 1925
(pregnant w/Helga at time)

'A nurse came in and told me they were ready to see me downstairs. I look at my mother, nod my head and I start to leave.'

"Helga darling!" my mother calls out. "Come back one moment, my dear child."

I turn around. "What is it, mama?"

"I want to give you a kiss."

"But I'll be right back. They just want me for a moment."

"I know, Liebchen, I know. Just come here and give your mother a kiss first."

I went back to her bedside. My mother hugs me tightly and kisses me several times. Then I go off with the nurse.

'During a long consultation with my doctors, I am suddenly seized by an overwhelming sense of fear and dread concerning my mother. I break down in hysterical screaming. When the nurses all ask what's the matter, I cannot tell them. I don't really know.

'Upon arriving back on my mother's floor, I overhear two nurses talking about a woman who's just died. I didn't realize immediately, it was my mother.

'When a doctor finally comes and tells me, I beg them to let me see her and they show me her body. Her neck is covered in bandages all soaked in blood. Oh, how I cried and screamed! I was inconsolable. That damned doctor! Everyone he operated on died. He killed my mother as sure as if the Nazis had shot her. I'd heard about this doctor from several different people. My poor mother was another one of his victims.'

'They let me stay on at the hospital for a few days after my operation. I suppose they had no idea what to do with me. I was grief stricken over losing my mother. It was the worst pain I'd ever had to endure.

'Very soon after that a woman comes into my hospital room to see me. She is tall, with sturdy shoulders and a long fine neck. Her hair was swept up and tied in the back. She was not beautiful, in the classic sense, but she is very attractive. She has marvelous eyes, like a hawk. Her features are sharp and focused and her manner gives off incredible competence.'

"Hello Miss Helga, my name is Marie Albert." Her voice is firm and soothing. "I work for a man named Alfred Blum. Monsieur Blum runs several homes for Hebrew children here in Brussels. We are making arrangements for you to go into one of these homes. At least temporarily. What would you think of that?"

I wanted to say, I'd rather stay with my friend Ruthie. Instead I just nod and ask, "Where is it?"

"One is actually quite near to here. I could bring you around and introduce you maybe tomorrow? Are you feeling steady on your feet yet?"

'I assure Marie Albert that I am fine on my feet. I could tell right away all the nurses around me were very impressed with Marie Albert. And that she had taken an interest in my case. The reputation of Alfred Blum and Marie Albert was very high around town.

'They buried my mother, Elka Oling Wallnau, in the Jewish cemetery there in Brussels. Everything according to the Jewish faith. It's so sad to remember. Except,' Helga recalls with an impish twinkle. 'It's against Jewish law to be buried with any writing. But my mother had insisted she have the poem my father wrote to her from the camp. We put it in the casket with her.'

'The next day Marie Albert returned to the hospital to pick me up. Together we walk the several blocks over to one of the homes of Alfred Blum. It was a large brownstone, which had been chopped up into separate living quarters. The bottom floor had been made into an apartment for the couple who ran the home. This was where the children ate their meals. The couple was named Tiefenbruner. They were Orthodox Jews. The husband wore a yarmulke around the house. The couple celebrated all the religious holidays with strict observance.

'Mr. Tiefenbruner is a sweet, kind man. I can see right away it is he who enjoys caring for the children and seeing to their various needs and wants. His wife, Mrs. Tiefenbruner on the other hand, is many months pregnant and thus not quite in her right mind. She stays inside their apartment/room and hordes whatever food she can.'

On the walk over Marie Albert tells me, "You could be of some assistance to Mr. Tiefenbruner. His wife is too ill with her pregnancy. She can't be of much help to him."

"What could I do?"

"Well, for instance, some of the children will have medical appointments on one day. It is necessary for someone to accompany them to the hospital. Drop them off and bring them back home."

"Yes," I tell Marie Albert. "I'd be most happy to help."

Marie Albert smiles a tight close smile. It doesn't quite reach her lovely grey eyes, which always seem so serious. "That would please the Tiefenbruners greatly, my child." She looks at me. "You wouldn't be afraid to be out walking on the streets?"

"Oh no!" I answer her quickly. "I'm out on the street all the time."

Helga recalls, 'That really was the truth. I *was* out on the street all the time. Also this woman Marie Albert had impressed me greatly. Somehow right away I wanted very much to please her. I didn't even know why. She inspired such feelings in everyone.'

(Editor's note: In 1997 Marie Albert published a memoir of her time as the directress of a home for Jewish orphans in Wezembeek Oppem, a suburb of Brussels. The book is written in French and has never been translated into English. Her testimony has also been entered into the U.S. Congressional Record. The title is "A Reef of Hope".

Alfred Blum, pronounced "bloom", (eventual husband of Marie Albert) is also a central figure in the story. He was a director of the AJB (Assn. of Jewish Belgians) in Brussels during the occupation. As such he was directly accountable to the Occupiers for enforcing their "work orders", supplying the Nazis with lists of names and addresses of Jews destined for deportation.

The AJB employed a policy of "presence" and "choice of lesser evil" which amounts to the appearance of submission in order to increase chances of survival. Many Belgian Jews resented this relationship.

But in fact an internal squabble between levels of the Nazi ministry benefitted Blum and the AJB and gave Blum the ability to maintain several orphanages well into the summer of 1944.

Blum himself is arrested in September of 1942 along with five other AJB directors. They are sent to a transit camp to await transport to Auschwitz. After fifteen days the Belgian Queen Elisabeth and Vatican envoy Cardinal Van Roey lodge a formal complaint. That results in a major disagreement between Nazi departments followed by the relatively quick release of Blum and the other AJB members.

For some time after that the Nazis appear publicly concerned with the appearance of diplomacy and they tout Blum's orphanages and old persons homes as proof of their civility. But it is all for show. Nazi "work orders" are a euphemism for transport to extermination points. The problem for Alfred Blum and the AJB was being caught in the middle. Arrested by Nazis for "disloyalty", the AJB were also harassed by the remaining Jewish population for "not resisting hard enough".)

Below: Mademoiselle Marie Albert

Chapter Eight

Alfred Blum/A Round-Up

Helga goes on to say, 'There is very little food in the Tiefenbruner house. Mrs. Tiefenbruner, the pregnant wife, goes around looking weary and worn out from everything. She keeps a faded kerchief tied around her head for Orthodox modesty. Children run around everywhere under foot. Marie Albert showed up most mornings, like this one, with a sack full of groceries, which she leaves on the kitchen table. Herr Tiefenbruner, the husband, yarmulke on his head, carries one toddler in his arms, with another clinging to his ankle. He puts the one toddler down and exchanges a chaste hug with Marie Albert.

'The children all adore Herr Tiefenbruner. They pester the life out of him. And I never see him get cross with any of them ever. His wife is altogether different. She does her best to ignore the children as much as possible. In fact I see her eating food on several occasions that had been specifically prepared for the children. In her defense she was very pregnant. Some women go downright crazy.

'I'd been living there a week or so before I met Monsieur Alfred Blum. He came sweeping into the orphanage one morning like Father Christmas himself, handing out gumdrops to all the kids. His booming voice bellowed. His large loud laugh echoed throughout the rooms.' (Editor's note: The time is late fall of 1942. Helga does not know that Alfred Blum has recently been released from a Nazi camp after being held for two weeks.)

'Blum is handsome, somewhere in his late-thirties. He is not terribly tall, but not short either. His build is stocky almost fat, his suit is extremely well-tailored.

'Frau Tiefenbruner keeps trying to get his attention, attempting to tap him on the shoulder. But the children keep nudging her out of the way. She comes close to losing her patience.'

"Monsieur Blum! Monsieur Blum!" shouts Frau T. "The plumbing upstairs! It is very bad! Please! You really must send someone over today."

Blum breaks his attention away from the kids a moment. "I'll see to it!" Then he returns to the squealing children flocking around him.

"Please!" cries Mrs. Tiefenbruner. "Upstairs! Monsieur Blum!"

"Yes! Yes! Madame! Before I leave."

'The children continue to flock around Blum. They beg for more gumdrops. I glance over and suddenly notice Marie Albert watching the whole scene closely. I realize with a shock that Madamoiselle Marie Albert is completely in love with Alfred Blum. I've always been able to read certain things in people and I could tell that immediately about her.

'I had developed a crush on Marie Albert myself and so I knew, just by the way she looked at Blum. I knew by the way she watched him and anticipated what he might ask of her and the way she knew it almost before he did. I was wildly impressed by the both of them. What they were doing seemed so romantic and dangerous. Saving these poor Jewish kids! You see, somehow I still didn't consider myself one of them. But it seemed so masterful of Blum convincing the Nazi occupiers it was in their best interests to allow them to run these homes. To show the International Red Cross the names and ages of Jewish kids who were living in these homes.

'The real surprise would come later, after I met Marie Albert's sister and discovered that she too, was madly in love with Monsieur Blum.

'When he went upstairs to look at the plumbing, Marie Albert took me aside into the kitchen.'

"How's it going for you here, Helga?" she asks as she puts the groceries away.

"Just fine," I answer, also helping with the groceries.

"Your leg is feeling better then?"

"Oh yes, much better. Thank you."

"Well in that case, maybe you would like to take some of the children to their doctor's appointment on Thursday? We have three or four scheduled already."

"Oh yes, Madamoiselle! I'd love to do that."

Marie Albert smiled that taut smile. She looks at me closely. "They must all wear their yellow stars. And have them visible." She pauses. "You too Helga."

"Yes, ma'am." I say softly just a few seconds before Blum bursts back into the room.

"Damn!" he says. "I have to tell you I'd have made a half decent plumber myself!" His jacket is off, and the sleeves of his white dress shirt are rolled up to his elbow.

"You were able to fix it, Alfred?" asks Marie Albert.

"Of course!" Blum's voice booms. "Now? Where's my coffee and pastry?" And he laughs. His voice is full of merriment, as if every plumber in Belgium is always served coffee and pastry at every job.

I look over at Marie Albert. "If there's any pastry around," I say. "Frau Tiefenbruner will have sniffed it out by now."

Blum laughs again. "So?" His large voice sounds trapped in the small room. "Is our dear Helga not the little dormouse we suppose her to be?"

Marie Albert looks at me. "Don't forget dear, Frau Tiefenbruner is eating for two."

"At least," Blum interjects sending a wink in my direction.

I giggle. But I didn't have the nerve to tell them, Frau Tiefenbruner ate the food meant for the children as well as her own food. Maybe they knew? I don't know. I wouldn't have cared so much if she'd been nice about it or even embarrassed. But she seemed to act as if she was entitled somehow.

Marie Albert tells Blum that I will take the children to the hospital on Thursday.

"Excellent! Excellent!" says Blum. "You can bring them in the morning and either Marie or I will collect them in the afternoon. That way you don't have to wait around the hospital all day." He pauses. "You're not afraid to be out in the streets?"

"No, monsieur. I am not afraid." I wish I could have told him why, but in truth I didn't know.

"Excellent! I tell you, underneath their swastikas, Nazis are as easily manipulated as anyone else." He laughs his big laugh, as if someone had told him a great joke."

"Alfred," Marie Albert intones. "We're running late now."

"Yes, yes, okay Marie. Well, keep yourself safe, Helga Wallnau. Don't wrestle Frau Tiefenbruner for any crumbs." He smiles at me. "This is just temporary. We're going to bring you out to the big house. As soon as we make a place for you."

Helga pauses before she continues, 'On that Thursday morning I'm standing in the foyer surrounded by five young children all dressed in coats, all with the yellow stars plainly visible. Monsieur Tiefenbruner, smaller than his wife and thin like a reed, fusses with the children's buttons and scarves.

"Now don't hide your star, Helga," says Tiefenbruner. "That's the Star of David. The greatest of the Hebrew kings. King David had no fear. He felled the giant Goliath."

'I nodded. I couldn't tell him I hated that hideous ugly star. That it meant nothing to me whatsoever.'

"Now Helga dear," adds Tiefenbruner. "Be sure you come right home after you drop the children off. Mrs. Tiefenbruner could use your help this afternoon and we don't want to be worrying where you are."

(Editor's note: The six-inch yellow six-pointed star, with a "J" in the center had been imposed in Belgium six months earlier. The imposition of the stars caused great unrest among the Jewish population. Many non-Jews began wearing the star not realizing it was the preliminary step in deportation. Blum's AJB were responsible for distribution of the actual cloth stars and Alfred

Blum himself wrote a general letter urging compliance with the orders, to register, and wear the star or risk grave consequences for your families.)

Helga continues, 'This morning with the kids, I was happy to get out of the house. As always. It didn't matter to me what house really. I never liked being cooped up inside anywhere. No matter the streets were full of Nazis who wanted to kill me. I was seventeen! It was all a great adventure. The children were always very obedient, and I was excited to be out on the street by myself.

'I was already thinking maybe I could steal some time today, after I dropped the children off? No one would expect me home too terribly soon. Marie Albert and Blum were going to pick them up, so I was free. And there was my favorite department store, Bon Marche. It was right there on the way back home. I could slip inside for a brief time and browse around. Not that I had any money, you understand. Just to see what was in the store these days. You realize, my family was in the clothing business. I'd always had the finest things to wear. I just wanted some time to myself. Some time that was completely my own.

'And so I did just that! I stole time! After bringing the children safely to the hospital, I slipped away back to the department store. It was a huge store, like a Macy's. And always one of my favorites. Both my mother's and mine! I couldn't resist.

'It was obvious the store was having trouble keeping the shelves stocked. There was just very little merchandise available these days. Still I was in my glory, looking over everything and anything that caught my attention. I watch the store clerks outfit a mannequin for one of the windows. I float down the aisles drinking in all the lovely displays. I try on some hats and draw the attention of a saleslady. She gets excited for a moment until she realizes I'm only shopping. Not buying.

'Yet for me it didn't matter. Inside that store I was completely transported out of the war. It didn't matter the shelves were only half-full. It didn't matter that I had no money to spend. It was crazy! But all the while I was shopping amidst all these wonderful things I couldn't buy, everything that was happening drifted away. The war. My mother dead. My father, who knows where? It all drifted right out of my head. I didn't give a thought to the Tiefenbruners or the children or anything.

'After quite some time I catch sight of a clock and I realize it's even later than I thought. I start to look for an exit. After I adjust my handbag to cover the dreaded star, I go out the closest door. It opens right out on the main plaza of town. And I am totally astonished to find that I've walked directly into a Nazi round-up.

'Soldiers have just swept through an apartment building two doors down from the store. They have put up sawhorse barricades and a processing station consisting of two long rectangular tables where officers are taking down information from detainees. These people mill about, jostling each other in a state of agitated fear. All of them exhibit their dingy yellow stars sewn on their chests. Some of these people have already been loaded into the paddy-wagon vans waiting with the back doors open.

'Anyone without the papers of a Belgian Christian was going into the police trucks. My first thought was, "Oh no! Marie Albert and Blum! They're going to know I stole time. They'll find out I disobeyed. That I did not come straight home. Now get this, my fear wasn't that these men were going to take me to the death camps. Forget that! I was afraid of my friends finding out what I'd done. Stealing time in the department store!

'My God!' exclaims Helga. 'I was so out of it!'

'The round-up was a scene of chaos barely under control. Ten Nazi guards in helmets with guns and dogs are standing around smoking cigarettes. Meanwhile fifty or so civilians, men and women, both young and old are all shouting and arguing, pushing and shoving one another. They are in fearful protest over the whole affair. There are no young children that I can see.

I snug up my handbag tight and keep walking forward. There is no chance now to turn around without looking conspicuous. I know that. My breathing I fight to control as I check the faces of these Nazi officers, I'm looking for one who might be easier.

'Finally I stride boldly up to one officer who is standing beside the sawhorse barricade. This Nazi is in the midst of questioning an elderly man who appears confused and is emptying his pockets onto the table. Coins are rolling off onto the street.

"Hello?" I call out loudly. "What is all this here?" I use an upper class high German accent.

The Nazi looks at me. "Your identity card please, Fraulein."

"Yes, of course," I answer impatiently and start to dig around in my pocketbook. "The thing is I'm late!" I tell the Nazi. "My boss is going to fire me. I was supposed to be back in the office ten minutes ago." I try to catch eye contact with him.

The Nazi seems to show a trace of sympathy.

I pretend to keep looking for the card as I say, "You see I work just right there in the next block. I can't be late! Please, I've got to get through here!"

The officer nods his head, "Yah, Fraulein, but I still need to see-"

And at that precise moment another Nazi some yards away calls out this one's name. "Hey! Achtung, Heinrich! Obersturnfurher Kurt wants to see you!" He points to another group of officers standing off to the side.

The Nazi in front of me freezes at the sound of his name. He looks nervous right away and calls back, "You sure? What does he want with me?"

"Who knows!" the first one shouts back. "Just get your ass over here! Schnell!"

'The officer in front of me starts to lose his composure. His eyes dart around. He flexes his shoulders nervously and pulls his uniform straight. I watch him closely. The instant he turns to find the Obersturnfurher, I clutch my handbag tight and sidestep around the sawhorse barricade. Then I do not look back. I just continue walking away. Not running. But walking quickly.

'If that superior hadn't called him over, I don't think I'd be sitting here telling you any of this. But the poor guy got rattled, his superior wanted to talk to him.' Helga laughs. 'Any time you tell a German their superior wants to see them, ho! They melt away.'

Helga pauses thoughtfully. 'It's your fear that gets you killed, Jeffrey. Your fear stirs fear in the other person. I always believed that I could touch the soul of anyone on the street who wanted to harm me.'

'I arrive back home to find Mrs. Tiefenbruner in the kitchen. She is smearing the children's peanut butter on some crackers and stuffing them into her mouth. I apologize for being late and I tell her about the round-up. But not about the visit to the department store. "...I slipped through their clutches like a little cockaroach (sic)."

Mrs. Tiefenbruner looks fearful. She stops eating a moment. "A full round-up? Oh dear God! We heard they'd started that business now. In the Jewish areas. Let's pray the children arrive back home safely."

'I heard her words but had trouble believing her heart was in them. Frau T. wouldn't have missed those kids one bit. It was Herr Tiefenbruner, that it would've killed. Thankfully sometime later Marie Albert brought the children home all safe and sound. She had heard about the round-up.

"Thank God, you're safe!" says Marie Albert upon hearing my story. "My child!" She hugs me a moment. "What an experience! You showed very quick thinking. The streets are suddenly much more dangerous now. Everything has been accelerated. We will bring you out to the other home very soon. It will be easier for you out there, Helga."

*

'Oh, how I loved Madamoiselle Marie Albert! She seemed so tough and fearless. But somehow you knew underneath she had emotions. She even took me to a famous singing teacher there in Brussels. This man Swenenberg, he was known throughout Europe. I'd been singing since I was small and I knew I had a good voice. I'd begged to be taken for lessons.

'He lived in a lovely house all very nicely appointed. He brought me into the study and listened to me sing. I don't remember what song it was. Afterwards he sat down at the piano and said to me, "Now improvise." But I couldn't. That was that. But he told me, "You have gold in your throat, child. Now go home and learn your notes. You have a fine voice. But I don't teach music theory."

'I never did learn to read notes.

'Some weeks after that I moved out to Wezembeek Oppem, to the main home of Alfred Blum's, which was run and managed by Marie Albert. It was a huge building that resembled a school or a hotel. And it was some distance from town, almost to the end of the suburban train line. If you missed that second to last stop you had to walk back through the forest for about a mile to get to the home.

'That first morning at the home in Wezembeek, the first person I met was Dina, the assistant cook.'

(Editor's note: Historical records indicate that the Nazis raided the home in Wezembeek, just a short time before Helga came out to live there. The Nazis showed up unannounced and took everyone except those with Christian identity cards. Marie Albert was arrested along with forty or so children. During the course of the arrest Madamoiselle Albert managed to slip a piece of paper with a phone number into the hand of one of those not arrested. The number was for an aide to Belgium's Queen Elisabeth, who would in turn intervene on behalf of Marie Albert and the children. They were all released just a few days later. This incident was more evidence of the split in Nazi thinking regarding public relations.)

Blum's Orphanage for Jewish Children at Weezembeck, outside of Brussels, Belgium 1942

Chapter Nine

"I Cook with Chemistry!"

Helga went on, 'After we ride the trolley almost to the end of the line, Marie Albert and I walk a few blocks, then we stop in front of this huge imposing mansion. But instead of entering through the front door, we duck around the side and come in through the kitchen, where we encounter Dina. Somewhere in her mid-thirties, she has short brown hair which hangs limp around her pale features, a smallish face and large brown eyes. She is not unattractive, just a little mousey. However she wears an ill-fitting, drab peasant skirt and these clunky brown, old-fashioned boots, the kind that button up high over the ankle.

'Right away I thought, she could have been pretty, but her face looked perpetually tired and worried. Then too, of course there were those boots. Like something out the last century.

'Busy chopping vegetables, Dina pauses to greet me.'

Marie Albert introduces us. I try hard not to notice Dina's clunky boots. But it's hard. Marie Albert asks Dina, "Have you seen Felix? I must speak to him about the arrangements for Helga."

"No, ma'am, I've not seen him since early this morning." Dina's tone of voice was highly deferential, as was everyone who spoke to Marie Albert.

"I will bring the counselors in to meet you, Helga," says Marie Albert.

As soon as Marie Albert leaves the kitchen, Dina pulls out some bread and jam and offers me a slice.

'I like Dina immediately. She has huge warm brown eyes. Sort of sad and mysterious, I thought. Intelligent too though, you could tell. She wore not the slightest trace of make-up. She'd been a biochemist somewhere before the war. Of course, those boots were complete relics from the last century. But I would come to learn how the children of the home lying in their beds at night, they would hear those boots come clunking up the stairs. And they would call out to her.'

Dina stands there, a tall drooping willow, smiling with her huge eyes and perfect white teeth. I enjoy a bite of bread and jam, then I remark on how grand the house seems. "…It's practically a palace!"

Dina says, "Before Monsieur Blum bought it, this was a clinic for wealthy children with tuberculosis."

Helga continues, 'A moment later Marie Albert returns to the kitchen with the four female counselors of the home, whom she introduces to me one by one.

'First is Rosa, who vaguely resembles Maureen O'Hara, very beautiful with dark, lustrous hair and very Jewish-looking, like a girl right out of Israel. She was impeccably dressed. Her hair is so dark by nature it is almost blue. She has black eyes too and perfect body language. Sparse in her movements and her talk. Nothing wasted in word or deed. Rosa seems neutral, neither plus nor minus. She never upsets anyone. Ever. And she is close to the house doctor, Sonya, and the house manager Felix. Rosa stands very straight and stiff as she shakes my hand.

'Then came Brigette from a super wealthy Christian Brussels family. But she dressed like a tomboy in men's work clothes. She appears rough and burly, but her personality is warm and charming. You knew right off from the way she spoke, there was money there. But it obviously hadn't tainted her spirit. Brigette hugs me and says, "Welcome Helga."

'The other two counselors stayed in the background. Lily seems very introverted and Annie comes off as rather slow-witted or maybe just purposely shy.

"All right, ladies!" Marie Albert claps her hands. "Let's get the children ready for lunch. Helga, you can help Dina here in the kitchen. And please set a place for Monsieur Blum. He'll probably join us today."

'A few minutes later I'm chopping carrots and watching as Dina turns a giant pot roast. We are alone in the kitchen. Today I learned was the head cook's day off. I sniff the air and smile. "I haven't smelled pot roast like that since we left Berlin three years ago."

Dina nods her head. She measures several different spices very carefully. "Monsieur Blum likes his food," she says with a hint of sarcasm. I watch her add the spices and notice she doesn't taste anything.

"And you always have plenty?"

Dina nods again. "Up till now, yes. Monsieur Blum has good sources." Her tone was not quite complimentary.

"You mean-?"

"I mean nothing. Except we're lucky to have his generosity."

"Yes, indeed." I understood the shift in tone. It was always tricky talking about the Black Market.

'The children eat first under the counselors' supervision. Both Lily and Annie actually dine with them. The kids number about twenty-five, ranging in age from about five to fifteen, a fair mix of boys and girls. After the meal Annie and Lily lead the children out of the dining room.

'Dina and I proceed to clean up after them and reset the dining room for the adults. As we were dealing with the serving platters, reloading them for the next meal, Blum bursts into the kitchen with Felix the young house manager trailing behind. Felix looks impossibly young for his position, no more than sixteen. He was younger than I.

'Blum speaks over his shoulder. "Too lax, I tell you! You've got to crack the whip on them from time to time, Felix lad. Toughen them up a bit. Before the damn Nazis snatch them away to make soap out of them." Blum looks up and notices Helga. He softens his tone. "They need some discipline, Felix. After all, that's why we made you house manager."

Felix dips his head. "Yes sir, Monsieur Blum. I will initiate a little more discipline."

"Good! Good!" Blum lifts the cover off the pot roast and he smiles. "We don't want any of them running away for godsakes. But they must learn respect for other people's property and the like. Otherwise-" Blum sticks his finger in the pot and licks it. "Mmmm, they're no better than Nazis, right Helga?" He looks at me and I'm surprised. "Felix, this is Helga Wallnau. Helga this is Felix, our house manager. He rides herd on the children for us around here. If you have any trouble with any of them about anything, Felix is the one to see."

'Felix seemed far too young for such responsibility,' Helga recalls. 'He must've impressed Blum a great deal. He was handsome though not terribly big. But he was obviously strong-willed and tough minded, you could tell. There was great power to his personality. Everything stopped when Felix came into the dining room. I learned quickly that he and Doctor Sonya were very close. In fact they were in love.

'At the adult lunch table Blum presides as the patriarch. He quizzes everyone regarding their particular functions in the household. I watch Rosa. She eats her lunch with impeccable manners, a stiff back and absolute decorum, while Brigitte with her casual clothes appears entirely relaxed and at ease. She even laughs and jokes with Blum.

"I passed your father coming out of the Building Commissioner's office the other day," Blum says to Brigitte. "He looked right through me." And he laughs.

"Oh Daddy's totally ashamed to be doing anything with the damned Nazis. He claims to be stalling them. But I think, not completely." Brigitte shows no trace of embarrassment.

"Nazis don't stall too easily," Blum replies. "They're a get it done yesterday bunch."

"But Daddy's such a hypocrite! He curses them all to hell, then he endorses their checks."

Rosa looks over at Brigitte. "Don't your parents worry that you work at the home here?" She meant about the danger of helping Jewish kids.

Brigitte laughs. "Well, I have to rebel somehow, don't I, dear Rosa? Working to help these poor children seems like the most wonderful slap in his face, now doesn't it?"

Blum roars with laughter at that. Marie Albert looks as serious as ever. Dina frowns in Blum's direction, until she notices me watching, then she sends me a wink. After the luncheon I help Dina with the washing up. We are alone again.

"So?" asks Dina. "Which do you suppose is the head counselor?"

"I'd say Brigitte. She's so funny and charming."

"Nope." Dina smiles, shaking her head.

"Well it's certainly not Annie," I say.

"No, poor dear Annie. She's so sweet," says Dina amused.

"And not Lily, she's too aloof. So it must be the gorgeous Rosa. She belongs in Hollywood," I tell Dina. "If she were in a movie, she'd be framed for murder and um, George Saunders, he'd have to prove her innocent."

"No, no," Dina smiles. "George Raft."

"Well," I admit. "Someone who resembles Blum then."

"Oh, but Monsieur Blum is already entangled."

"What do you mean?"

"Marie Albert and her sister. He's wooed them both."

"She has a sister?"

"Yes. A few years younger. They both adore Monsieur Blum."

I look at her curiously. "And the heat runs both ways?"

"Oh yes! Yes." It was obvious from her tone that she did not share their feelings. "Don't be fooled by him, dear Helga. The Nazis eat out of his left hand while the Resistance eats out of his right." She pauses. "Everyone knows that."

Just then Blum appears out of nowhere. "Everyone knows what?"

"That Rosa is the head counselor," answers Dina without missing a beat.

"What?" Blum looks at me. "You don't think the beautiful princess Rosa is worthy?" I just giggle, embarrassed by Blum's attentions. "Okay, my dear," he says to me softly. "You'll be much happier out here. When you've finished with this, find Felix and he'll introduce you to your roommates."

'Sometime later I search out Felix and find him in the dormitory wing, where he is disciplining a boy of nine or ten for some infraction. The child kneels on the bare floor facing the corner. I watch for a moment, thinking, if Dina feels Blum is too close to the Nazis, what must she make of this? Felix, as I would come to see, could be as harsh as I imagined the Nazis to be.

'When he notices me, he comes over. "Hello Helga, give me a minute and I'll show you where your room is located." Then he turns back to the delinquent boy and barks, "You! Don't move a muscle! Till I return! Understood?"

The boy didn't budge.

Once out of the room, I ask, "What did the poor fellow do?"

"Him? Oh, he likes to play doctor with the little girls. I have to watch him all the time."

'We turn down several hallways, and wind up in the girls' wing, where Felix ushers me into a room with one double bunk bed and one single bed. They put me in with two girls close to my own age, though a little younger. Fernande slept in the upper bunk bed, while I was to take the lower. She has a contorted face, sunken, almost like a mushroom and she wears wooden clogs that go "clip-clop" all through the house. This girl never smiled. Not once! That I ever saw.

'The other girl Miriam is a stunning beauty! She is every bit as beautiful as Rosa, but in a different way. Miriam was just perfect looking in every way. And all she does is smile. She seems remarkable that way, all the time smiling.

'The head cook when I meet her is as fat as a dumpling and mean as pitch. Even so she sings like a nightingale. And she makes poor Dina do everything she doesn't feel like doing herself. Cook comes in and sees Dina, how she's measuring everything so precisely, and cook shouts, "What are you doing there now? Are you having a moment, darling?"

'And Dina would blink her large eyes nervously and shout back, "Leave me alone! I cook by chemistry! I'm a chemist, for godsakes!"

"Then why are you in my kitchen?" cook shouts back. "We're making stew, not bombs!"

'On Dina's day off, the cook would often keep herself locked up inside the kitchen alone. With an actual lock on the door! She'd come out for one minute while she brought the meal out, then she'd lock herself back up inside the kitchen with the food.

Towards the end food got scarce and we got so hungry, I thought of Uncle Walter's curse all the time. How he'd said, "You should learn how it feels to be hungry someday."

'I came to understand how everyone loved Dina. She hands out jam sandwiches to the children, behind the cook's back. And also how everyone both loves and fears Marie Albert, who stands for absolute discipline. One evening a few of the older children went down to the train station meet Marie Albert who was coming back late from town. When she saw the welcoming committee there to greet her, she scolded them, "What are you all doing here? It's far too late for you to be roaming around. You should all be in bed!" Marie Albert was all about efficiency. There'd been no need for anyone to meet her, so why were they there?

'Four or five months after I moved in, the Nazis came for an inspection.'

Chapter Ten

The Nazis Count the Children

'Marie Albert comes hurriedly into the kitchen one morning, as Dina and I are cleaning up from the children's breakfast. "I just spoke with one of our friends," she stresses the last word. "The Nazis will be out today to count the children. It is to be a surprise visit."

Dina's head swivels towards me immediately.

"So, we will all act surprised," Marie Albert continues. "And yes, Helga must hide while they're here. Along with young Franz. And that other little boy who came last week, Alex. Everyone else should be okay. Let me gather Rosa and Brigitte and I'll explain what we're going to do." With that she rushed back out of the kitchen.

"Your name is not on the official list of children who live here," Dina explains to me. "That's why we have to hide you. Otherwise they might take you off."

"Really? That has happened before?"

"Only once. They really did come by surprise. And they took everyone!" Dina brightens. "But see? We got a warning this time. Thank God!"

Marie Albert returns a few minutes later with Rosa, Brigitte and Felix trailing behind her.

"I have no idea why they picked today," Marie Albert explains. "Just be thankful we were warned. Now I suggest Helga, Franz and little Alex hide up in the attic linen storage. I think that's the safest place for them."

Brigitte pipes up. "Mademoiselle Albert? I could take the three on a long hike in the forest? Completely far away from here?"

"We considered that, Monsieur Blum and I. But there's the chance that someone sees you and reports it. Then we would face the questions and all."

Felix says, "What if they decide to search the attic anyway?"

Marie Albert responds sternly, "We'll just have to see to it they don't."

"But-" Felix starts to argue.

Marie Albert cuts him off. "Sorry Felix, we're not going to shoot any Nazis today."

"But what if-"

"Felix, please! Now Brigitte, you and Helga must go up and check out that attic linen storage. We must find a method to help Helga get up that ladder. Then we must make it as comfortable as possible. You might be up there for some time."

'When it came time for us to go up there into the attic, the two young boys look scared. Felix found a wide ladder, but it still gives my bad leg trouble. Felix helps hoist me up. Inside the attic room, the air is close and hot. Marie Albert escorts us up and tries to reassure our fears. "We'll get you all on the official list as soon as it's possible. But for now, you must hide. Be as quiet as you can."

Several hours later all the children are assembled in the front courtyard of the home. Four Nazi officers in their glistening uniforms and six soldiers in their green drab coats are checking the children off by name, one by one, against their official list. Off to the side stands Marie Albert with Rosa and Brigitte and Doctor Sonya. The doctor is smiling wearing her white physician's smock.

"They think they've surprised us," Doctor Sonya murmurs under her breath. "We're lucky."

"Yes," replies Marie Albert. "But like Alfred says, 'Money goes further than luck'."

One of the officers comes up to the women. "We would like now to see inside the premises, if you please, Mademoiselle Albert."

Marie Albert leads the parade of Nazi officers and soldiers on an exhaustive search of the home. In her usual efficient manner she has them poke their noses into every nook and cranny on each floor, before they lumber up to the next. The Nazis appear conscientious at first, but as the search wears on they begin to loosen up and start joking with each other out of boredom.

By the time they reach the landing directly below the attic linen storage, there are only two senior officers and three soldiers left. The rest have gone back downstairs to enjoy some coffee and pastry arranged by the cook. Rosa and Brigitte stay with Marie Albert and the soldiers. The Nazis, all except the one lieutenant in charge, seem anxious to join their comrades. They shift their weight from foot to foot and sigh heavily.

"What's up there?" snaps the lieutenant pointing to the attic door.

"All the winter quilts and winter bedding," Marie Albert replies. "We've had no need of them so far this season."

The officer looks at her a moment, then he goes over to inspect the wooden ladder attached to the wall. He runs his index finger along one of the rungs. It comes away dusty.

"This is the only access?" he asks.

"Yes," answers Marie Albert.

The Nazi lifts his boot onto the first rung of the ladder. All three women keep their faces perfectly still. The wooden rung creaks and groans as the officer hauls his full weight onto it. The second rung squeaks as well. His boots have trouble gaining purchase as the ladder is so close against the wall.

"Okay, Dieter!" the fellow officer chides. "No more schnitzel for you. Don't break their ladder now." The soldiers laugh.

The lieutenant stands on the second rung, obviously debating whether to continue further up. He looks at Rosa. "What is up here, exactly?"

"Heavy woolen quilts. Comforters. Pillows. Blankets. Towels." Her voice is perfectly even and calm.

"All Blum's gold," quips the other Nazi officer. "Dieter! You think it's your lucky day?"

Brigitte looks up. "Be careful about the rats up there, sir. I know Felix set a trap last year."

"Is it big enough?" cracks one of the soldiers. Everyone laughs. The ladder rung bearing the Nazi gives another serious creak, as if it's about to break.

Helga recalls, 'Up there in that attic storage, only a few feet away from them all, we could only hear muffled voices and heavy boots. The boot sounds had gotten louder and louder and the voices clearer, the closer they came.

'By the time they were right below us, I'd gathered a frightened little Alex up next to me and wrapped us all up in blankets and quilts. Alex begins to cry and whimper and I had to cover his mouth gently. I whispered to him. Then we all held our breaths. There was nothing else to do. We listened to the blood rushing in our ears.

'At last the Nazi leaped down from the ladder. Maybe he saw himself crashing down? They all left shortly after that. Felix had brought a wide portable ladder to help me up there. He brought it back to get us all down.

'Once they'd gone everyone assembled back in the kitchen, Marie Albert, Rosa, Brigitte, Doctor Sonya and Felix. These last two seem exuberant. Though there is a spirit of joy and relief throughout the room. Everyone also looks slightly exhausted.

"I wonder what they would've done to us?" says Doctor Sonya. "If they'd found them."

"We'd have been arrested too, I'm sure," says Brigitte.

"But worse for Helga and the boys," Felix interjects.

Brigitte looks over to Helga. "Were you terrified up there?"

"A little," I answer, mostly to be agreeable.

"Only a little?" Brigitte smiles.

Helga shrugs. "When Alex began to cry. I thought maybe you could hear?"

"She's fearless! Our little Helga!" Dina cries proudly.

Felix smiles deeply into the eyes of Doctor Sonya. "Wasn't it smart how I dusted the rungs of that ladder? It looked like no one had been up there in months."

"That was inspired," says Marie Albert.

Doctor Sonya beams a loving smile back at Felix. That's when I begin to realize it's really deep and serious between these two.

"Well that Nazi wasn't going to make it all the way up anyway," Felix adds with a twinkle in his eye. Everyone looks at him curiously. "I weakened the last rung of that ladder completely. It would've never taken his full weight."

Everyone laughs at that.

"Okay Felix," says Marie Albert. "You've earned a beer for that one."

Dina leans in close to me. "You're so brave, Helga. You must come shopping with me next time. I won't be so afraid."

"I'd be happy to come with you. I love to shop!"

They all look over at me as if gauging my courage.

Marie Albert says, "You may accompany Dina on her shopping trip, Helga. But you must both show your stars at all times. And be careful."

Dina looks pleased and she hugs my arm close.

*

'Following the Nazi inspection life took on a certain routine around the home. I was assigned to help Dina in the kitchen. I quickly came to realize she was the rock upon which the children depended for comfort and sustenance both.

'In the mornings I lie still in my bed and listen while Fernande clip-clops and Miriam pads around the room. They both get dressed early and have duties dealing with getting the children up and dressed. I slide out of bed after they've gone, get myself dressed and go down to the kitchen. Dina was often making porridge for the children's breakfast.

'She would set me down to buttering a small mountain of toast. After watching me a moment or two she comes over.

"Darling Helga, we don't have all morning," she says gently as she picks up a slice of toast. "Now there's an intelligent, efficient method for everything, even buttering toast."

'And she takes the knife, dabs on some butter and in one swift precise motion spreads a light even coat across the toast. She repeats the motion on another piece, then hands the knife back to me.

'I wanted to tell her, I'd had a nanny to butter my toast for me. But I couldn't somehow. Dina came from such poverty, I felt guilty telling her such things. Plus I would've had to tell her how horrible that nanny was. How she whipped me with that "cat of nine tails". I just couldn't tell her all that.

'A young boy of seven or so comes bursting into the kitchen obviously looking for a treat before breakfast. The head cook was busy at her desk over in the corner. But she catches sight of the little urchin and shouts, "Shoo now! Scoot! You wait for your breakfast like all the other children."

'The boy stops dead in his tracks and starts to turn around. Dina comes over and escorts him back through the door. She manages to slip him a morsel of toast in the process. That was Dina.

'A minute later the cook gets up to check on Dina's porridge. She dips a spoon in and tastes it. "Oh no! Far too sweet! How much sugar did you put in there? The whole month's ration?"

Dina comes over and looks at the porridge bubbling away in the giant pot. "It looks fine. And I use a little molasses instead of straight sugar. The children love it."

"Well who told you to do that?" The cook put her hands on her hips.

"No one told me! I cook the way I cook! By color and chemistry. I can tell if something is right by how it looks in the pot. I don't need to taste it every two minutes."

Cook throws her hands up. "Good God in heaven! I've never heard anything so crazy in all my life."

I stifle a laugh. Suddenly Blum pops into the kitchen; he's looking for the cook. He pauses at the pot of porridge, sticks his finger in and tastes it.

"Mmmm! Delicious, cook!" And at that the cook perks up and beams proudly. "The children must love it!" adds Blum.

"Yes, they do," Dina interjects flatly. The cook ignores her and proceeds to fawn over Blum. He appears to have something important to discuss with her.

'After breakfast Dina and I wash up the dishes and pots together. I notice Dina's long slender, finely shaped fingers and the rough redness of the skin due to her scullery work.

"Your poor hands," I say. "They look terrible! You must use some lotion."

Dina examines her hands a moment. "I haven't had any hand cream for months and months." She pauses. "These hands weren't made for kitchen work. I'm a trained chemist. I taught at the University. Before all this insanity."

'I realized Dina had been educated at a very high level. And I suddenly understood her faintly hostile, superior attitude towards both Blum and Marie Albert. They were management. Dina was labor. But in the normal scheme of things, back before this insanity as she called it, she would've been above them in the social hierarchy. Blum depended on Marie Albert to run the nuts and bolts of the home, to pay the bills and keep everything going. And yet Dina was the rock solid foundation on which the whole atmosphere of the home depended. If Marie Albert was the brains, Dina was the heart.

'At night I would lie in bed and hear those footsteps, Dina's ancient boots, as she trudged up the stairs. Those clunky boots echoed behind her. Her steps always sound slow and bone-weary. I can picture her, tall but slightly stooped. She carries a glass of milk. The house is completely dark and quiet, except for those boots of Dina's clumping up the stairs.

'Invariably at that moment a child's voice rings out. "Dina! Dina!"

'The footsteps stop. I know she listens for exactly where the voice is coming from, then she turns in that direction. "Yes, my darling, I'm coming."

'Dina was everything to those children, especially the younger ones. And they adored her. She was their joy in the daytime and their comfort at night. No matter how late in the night. Dina always came, she never refused them. No matter how tired or exhausted she was, Dina answered their cries in the night. Dina always came to comfort them.

'The children hated her days off. Marie Albert took over her duties, but everything was different. No secret treats. No comfort in the night. Where Dina indulged them, Marie Albert disciplined. It was a boot camp atmosphere when Marie Albert was in charge. No secret jam sandwich treats. No comfort for bad dreams in the middle of the night.

'On her days off Dina always smuggled out a little package of food to her starving parents, who were in hiding in town. My heart went totally out to her.'

Editor's note: In her memoir "A Reef of Hope", Marie Albert Blum writes that she kept the children busy with schooling and light household and yard chores. In general older children looked after younger ones. Within the context of the home she created a "cocoon" which sheltered them as much as possible from the danger outside. Ms. Albert believed it best to try to insulate the children from the atrocities being committed on the outside. Thus it was part of her management style to keep discipline sharp and everyone on their routine. Marie Albert because of her closeness to Alfred Blum knew better than anyone how easily it could all turn bad. She understood that the Nazi regime was merely playing a public relations game so as to appear civilized in their occupation. For the Nazis it was only a game. Blum and Marie Albert knew full well if the Allied push inland started to succeed, the Nazi's so called "final solution" would escalate. No one would be safe anywhere.

Chapter Eleven

Shopping With Nazis

'Just before lunch one day, I am peeling carrots for the stew, when Felix comes into the kitchen accompanied by my cousin Bernie Oling. "Hello Helga, my sweet cousin!" Bernie exclaims. "Here you are!" And he glances around in wonder, as if he'd never seen a kitchen before. "Hey, this place doesn't look so bad."

Dina breaks out some tiny pieces of fruitcake, which she serves with some coffee. Bernie thanks her and says to me, "I've brought you a letter from your father. It comes from one of the Nazi camps." He hands me a letter with a stamp that bears Hitler's picture. "Actually, your father Uncle Hans sent it to his brother Paul in Zurich. Paul sent it on to me here. For you."

'I took the letter and put it in my pocket.

"Aren't you going to read it now?" Bernie sounds surprised.

"No. I'll read it later. Thank you for bringing it all the way out here, cousin."

He nods his head. "I've heard from Uncle Erich too. He and Aunt Molly are now settled in New York. Uncle Martin has made it as well. Your father's brother Walter Wallnau, he's in a camp somewhere. I'm sorry to tell you, cousin."

"How do you know all this?"

"From the man running your business in Berlin. They've been in touch with me, since your dear mother passed."

"What about Aunt Frieda? What's happened to her?"

Bernie dips his head. "We don't know for sure." He pauses. "I'm sorry, cousin."

My eyes fill with tears. I couldn't help it. I couldn't look at my cousin either.

"The man in Berlin," Bernie continues. "He keeps asking if we've found the patterns for that three-piece suit? I thought you might have found them among your dear mother's papers."

I don't answer. I was still thinking of Frieda. She was so dear to me.

"Those plans could mean a good deal of money, Helga."

I look at him now. "You mean if I were to hand them over to you, cousin?"

"What? You don't trust me? I wouldn't cheat you, Helga. Besides, don't you think your father would like to see his idea come to fruition?"

I stay firm. "When father returns he will do what he's going to do."

Bernie looks curious. "Then you do have the plans?"

"No! I don't know if I do or not. I haven't even been through all of my mother's papers."

'Dina hears all of this and she invites Bernie to stay for lunch. He declines claiming he must return to work. But he is very vague about for whom he works. Tailoring on the Black Market? Doing side work for the Nazis maybe? Who could blame him? Everyone has to eat.

'After Bernie leaves, I can't think of anything except Aunt Frieda and Uncle Walter. Both of them, like Josi. And my father. Prisoners in the death camps. Somewhere?

What about the diamond Erich had given Frieda?

'The letter from my father burned in my pocket. But I didn't want to open it. I wanted to savor the feeling. After we cleaned up the lunch, Dina asks about it. I pull out the letter and begin to read it, with Dina there. Father expresses his sorrow about the death of my mother. The great love of his life. He encourages me to keep on with my studies. He assures me the man in Berlin will still help me. Everything is upbeat and positive. There is nothing about any gas chambers or any of that.

'Dina comes up behind me. She has been looking over my shoulder. "Oh! What magnificent handwriting! Your father must be quite sensitive. And intelligent."

"You read handwriting?" I ask.

"Oh yes! My grandmother was a gypsy."

'I hand her the letter, which she studies for a long time.

"He sounds like such a wonderful man," says Dina. "I can see quite a lot about him from this sample. He would like to change the world, your father." She pauses. "But he is not so good with the money, I think."

I laugh. "You can see all that? You might be right. Uncle Erich is the businessman in the family."

"But your father is much more than a mere businessman. Look at his 'm' and his 'w', the shape and the curls. He's a bit of a dreamer with lots of imagination. Charming and graceful. A musician perhaps?"

I howl with glee. "Yes! Yes!" I was thrilled. "You're quite good with that stuff."

*

'The following week I go shopping in town with Dina. We take the train all the way to the open-air marketplace. Despite Marie Albert's warning I still conceal my yellow star under my large handbag. Dina hides her star too, but she's more fearful in her attitude. We are on the train with Nazi soldiers and even an officer or two and many of them get off to shop with us at the market.

'No one looks too concerned about anything. The stalls of the marketplace appear vastly depleted and the vendors all look depressed. Dina and I sort through oranges looking for the sweet ones.

"I think you were right to hold onto those designs, Helga," Dina says to me. "Your father will be pleased to have them when he returns."

I look at her closely. "So you believe my father will come back?"

"Oh yes, I do! It can't go on like this forever. The world will not support it. This genocide. Not forever! Are they going to stand by and let the Nazis kill every single person of Jewish origin?"

'Some of the shoppers near us move away. Dina doesn't say anymore.

'It wouldn't be too long before I would come to realize that poor Dina had somehow fallen completely in love with my father. A man she had never even met! From his letter. From his handwriting. And from all the stories I'd told her about him. How he used to race his Essex Super Six in rallies down the highways. She begins to speak about meeting him and getting to know him, almost as if in her head, she imagined them married.

'I was already terribly fond of Dina and I could never tell her she didn't stand a chance with my father. She was like a frightened rabbit. Whenever I made the slightest inquiry into her romantic life, she would roll her eyes back and hide behind that mysterious smile. Dina had a heart of pure gold and the kindest loving spirit you could imagine. But she had no sense of fashion or style. Those clunky boots! Who could get past them? Boots that laced up high over the ankle, like boys wore. No sense of class or upbringing. My father would've considered her a farm girl, at least in my imagination. But I could never tell her any of this.'

'That first day after shopping we were each carrying several bags of groceries as we made our way along the street back towards the train station. About twenty yards from the station we pass a group of five or six Nazi soldiers standing around smoking cigarettes. They point to us and jostle each other in a comradely manner.

'One of the bags I'm carrying suddenly gives out at the bottom and oranges go bouncing all over the ground. We both shriek! Then we laugh as we go chasing after the fruit.

'The Nazis watch our flurry of excitement with interest. But none of them offer any help. I hear one say, "Must've taken a suitcase full of ration tickets for all that. Shame to waste good food on dead people."

"No kidding!" says another. "Those two are doing somebody, no doubt."

"I don't recognize them from the usual bunch of Yid floosies." He casually removes his Lugar from its holster. Then he fires a shot a few feet away from Dina, who is too scared to scream. "Damn train depot rats!" And he laughs.

A second Nazi takes out his pistol. He fires a shot near my feet. Dina then grabs my hand and we start to run towards the train station. The Nazis each fire once more, not too close. We can hear them laughing as if it were some great sport.

'Somehow we made it safely onto the outbound train. We were completely out of breath, huffing and puffing, still clutching the bags of groceries. But we are smiling.

"My God!" I say. "I didn't think I could run like that."

"Nazi pigs! Sons of bitches!" Dina murmurs under her breath.

I gasp. "Dina!"

"What? Fascist thugs, Helga! They should be strung up by their private parts."

I laugh. "They were just trying to scare us, I knew that."

"You think that makes it better?"

"Better than being arrested," I say.

Dina looks at me closely. "You are truly something, Helga! I thought I'd wet my drawers, I was so scared."

I laugh again. "I just didn't want to lose the groceries. What would we have told Cook?"

Dina finally laughs. "We tell her she goes shopping next time."

"Oh, I'd go again!" I say. "I don't mind."

Dina looks stunned. "You! You're really not afraid of them, are you?"

"Of them? No. But I am scared of things. Blum scares me. And Marie Albert a little too. Even Felix sometimes. They all frighten me."

"But child, it's the Nazis who-"

"I know, I know. It's the Nazis who want to send us to the death camps. It's the Nazis I should be afraid of, I know that. Somehow I'm just not getting it."

Dina puts her arm around me. "I want you to come visit my parents with me sometime. They would love to meet you!"

*

'I agree to come out of curiosity. Everyone in the home knew Dina's parents lived in hiding. They were Yugoslav Jews. Just like everyone knew she squirreled away little bits of food for them.

'It was an afternoon some weeks later, we boarded the inbound train carrying little bundles of food under our coats. We rode the train together to a part of Brussels I didn't know at all. It was a ghetto of sorts. We both conceal our stars. It was a habit I couldn't break. Dina still seems timid and frightened, but she looks over to me and I smile. This is an adventure! I stand up straight and adopt an attitude that I belong just where I am.

'We scurry through the dirty, grimy streets of this area where Dina leads us into a rather rundown apartment building and up to an ugly stained apartment door. Our knock is answered by a frightened looking elderly woman who opens the door just a crack at first. Then she opens it wide and mother and daughter embrace. Dina quickly introduces me to her mother.

'Dina's parents live in dire poverty. Two rooms and a toilet room, which also serves as a kitchen. There were rats and vermin. These folks were basically starving, anyone could see. Educated people. Intellectuals! I was surprised, they'd not found a way out. They got so excited over the bits of food we'd brought, it was touching and stirred my heart. This was the typical sweet Jewish couple, right out of the ad for the diamond ring. If you follow my meaning? So charming and nice they were, it seemed a crime them being forced to live like this, like frightened mice in absolute squalor. We were there only five minutes and I wanted to leave.

'Dina proceeded to unwrap a small menorah and set the candles in for Hannakah. Her mother and father are over-joyed. It was December of 1943. I was embarrassed to admit, I hadn't remembered Hannakah. As I watched Dina's father prepare the little celebration, I remembered the young Gestapo who stopped me outside the theater that night. I was watching now what it meant to be Jewish. Still it seems completely foreign, completely alien to me. I just don't really get it.

'That day I was never so happy to get back to the home. I have to tell you, in that home during the Nazi time in Brussels, it was one of the happiest times of my whole life. As strange as that sounds, it's true. No one in the house feared me. No one tried to get anything out of me. With my bad leg I was the odd person out. All the time. But that was okay, I was always treated well by everyone.

'Around that time I was invited by the counselor Brigitte out to her family house for a luncheon visit. These people were super wealthy and their house was a genuine palace with servants. Her father was the head of some giant Belgian corporation.

'There was actual tension between Brigitte and her mother. I heard her mother scold her for her tomboy clothes and her klutzy sort of appearance. Brigitte had a fine figure. She could've looked like something out of Vogue magazine if she'd wanted. During the lunch there is a stiff cold atmosphere at the table, even between family members. Did that iciness come with such wealth, I wonder? Brigitte's father said some odd things about Monsieur Blum. It was obvious he didn't like him.

'This was the essential split in society during the Nazi time. Brigitte's Christian family in their splendid home and

Dina's Jewish family in their abject poverty. It was the general disruption and destruction of the European intellectual core. The super-wealthy went on with their clothes and their money, while the intellectuals were all hunted down and either killed or hounded out of their homelands. It was a time that worshipped mediocrity and conformity.'

Above: Alfred Blum circa World War I

Chapter Twelve

Blum and Marie Albert

'It was my spirit that saved me, I understood that. My "not-getting-it" gave me a unique insight into the whole experience. Maybe some of it had to do with being an adolescent. Years later this New York Jewish intellectual would tell me, "Helga, your energy is a gift from God. You should be speaking to groups."

'I knew what she meant. But there in the home during that time, I was like the princess. I had few responsibilities. And I was loved by all of them.

'A Russian woman had moved into the home recently with an entire wardrobe full of Paris fashions. She would offer to loan me anything, if I happened to go out for any sort of date or rendezvous. I had such a wonderful time just looking through all her lovely things.

'The home itself was a hotbed of intrigues! Picking up tidbits here and there, I could fantasize about Rosa and Brigitte and their romantic love lives. There was Blum and Marie Albert along her sister, whom I'd met now several times. In addition there was the plain and open affair going on between young Felix the house manager and Doctor Sonya. Even though she was so much older, it was obvious they'd fallen deeply in love.

'One day the following spring I am passing by the main office when Marie Albert emerges suddenly. She looks rather flushed and her clothes are slightly disheveled. I hear Blum's loud laughter echo from behind the door.

"Helga dear!" says Marie Albert almost smiling at the same time smoothing her dress.

"Oh, I'm sorry," I say slightly startled.

"For what, darling?"

"If I startled you, Mademoiselle Albert."

"Well," she says. "It looks as if I startled you."

I demur. "Yes, I guess you did."

Marie Albert smiles fully now. "That friend of your mother's called this morning. Madame Brotmann. She said she would try to come out today."

"Henne Brotmann? How wonderful!" I was thrilled.

'A few hours later a tall very stylishly dressed woman in her late thirties sits stiffly at the kitchen table of the home. A round tin, of the kind which holds fancy cookies, sits open between us. Dina serves Frau Brotmann some coffee.

'Henne Brotmann had been one of my mother's dearest friends here. I could tell she missed her nearly as much as I did. She'd come out several times, always with a large tin of fancy chocolate filled cookies. Everyone got very excited because it was the only time we ever saw anything chocolate. At least in the last year. Henne never stayed long. I thought seeing me maybe reminded her too much of what was now lost forever.

'Frau Brotmann gets up from the table and comes over to give me a hug and a kiss. "Helga darling, I won't be coming out anymore after today. We're moving somewhere safer. There is much talk of the Allies invading soon. This whole business could be over in six or eight months." She glances over Dina, who pretends not to be listening. "Do they plan to keep this place running? I mean, will Helga be safe here?"

Dina looks over. "I'm sorry ma'am, but Monsieur Blum does not confide his plans to me."

"No. Of course not. But everyone in town knows he has many important connections." She pauses. "On both sides."

"Doubtless, he does, ma'am. Yes," says Dina.

Henne Brotmann smiles at me. "He's marvelously clever, your Blum. He's convinced the Nazis to actually support these homes of his. To prove to the International Red Cross they're not gassing Jewish children to death." I look over to Dina, we share our surprise. "The Resistance is releasing information on the camps. They're using gas chambers now to kill Jews and others."

"Oh my father?" I gasp.

"Oh Helga, don't worry. If your father is still writing letters, he must've found a way to survive." I had told her of my father's letter.

Henne Brotmann leaves shortly after that. Dina comes and looks hard at the tin of chocolate cookies. "If you eat too many of those, you'll be sick in the night and have to visit Doctor Sonya."

I laugh. "Oh I couldn't do that. She's much too busy attending to Felix."

"Oh?" says Dina brightly, playing along. "Is Monsieur Felix still getting sick in the night?"

"Almost every night," I say. "From what I hear." And we both laugh.

"Good Lord," says Dina. "She could almost be his mother!"

I laugh. "I don't think Felix had a mother. He's too mean!"

"Oh Helga! Someone has to keep the children in line. Someone has to ride herd on them. Better that it's one of their own, right?" She meant Felix being so close to them in age. Besides the fact no one else was going to step up in that regard.

"I had a nanny who was mean like that, when I was little," I tell her. "A vicious monster! But my parents thought she was wonderful."

"Well Doctor Sonya thinks Felix is wonderful." Dina lowers her voice. "You mustn't tell a soul, but they're going to run off together. Don't say a word to anyone, Helga! But it's true." She pauses. "Helga dear, could you spare a cookie or two for my parents? They will faint dead away."

"Oh of course, of course, Dina dear."

'I was stunned to learn of Felix and Sonya's plan. Of course I promised not to tell. Whom did I talk to besides Dina anyway? Still, running off together! The two of them! It sounded so wildly romantic. It was an image I couldn't get out of my head. Every time I saw either of them, I had trouble looking them in the eye.

'That spring of '44 I visited Dina's parents in hiding several times. My skin crawled every minute we were in that apartment. I could practically feel the bugs and rats scurrying about underfoot. I couldn't understand how these two sweet intelligent people could put up with this squalor, the roaches, the bedbugs and God knows what else. I tried to imagine my own parents living there. In hiding! I think they'd have preferred death. I'm positive they would've!'

'We would slink around that ugly neighborhood, both of us carrying little bundles of food under our coats.

'I hated myself for thinking that way, but it's true! Was this what it meant to be Jewish? To be forced to live like this? In a total slum! By a world that hated the very sight of them? Them? No! Me too! You're one of them, Helga, I told myself. You must remember that. When are you going to get it? In my mind somehow I belonged with Brigitte and Marie Albert and Blum, though I knew Blum was Jewish, he never seemed typical. How was it I was one of these dreaded Jews? Of course I knew in my heart that I was. But still somehow I couldn't convince my brain. Not yet.

'On the last visit we made to her parents, I had to ride the train back to the home alone. Dina stayed behind with them, as she was off work the next day. I always rode the train with complete calm and confidence, my dingy yellow star hidden beneath the large square handbag, which I clutched tight to my side.

'That night the train was nearly empty. There were a few Belgian civilians, and a few young men who worked on the trains. They were riding to the end of the line. In addition there was a group of six or eight Nazi soldiers in their long green coats. There was a military installation there in Tervuren also near the end of the line.

'This was the last outbound train of the night. You must understand I adored riding the train. Everything about them! The big engines and the noise and the smell of the diesel. Everything! This particular night, I was exhausted and the gentle rocking motion of the train put me fast asleep. I slept right through my stop at Wezembeck Oppem, the stop for the home.

'I didn't awake until we pulled into the station at the end of the line. Now I would have to walk twenty minutes through the dark forest to get back to the home. Either that or two hours on the main road which took you far out of the way. Just the thought of it set ice crystals dancing in my hands and fingers.

'I sat there on the train a moment to gather my bearings. I watched the Nazi soldiers get off and the train employees. I waited until everyone was off before I stood up to get off the train. Once outside I stood there taking in some deep breaths. I did not want to appear to be in any hurry as I made my way out of the station. The trail leading into the woods was dark. There was no moon whatsoever.

"Hello?" one of the young train workers calls out to me. "May I be of some assistance?"

I turn with a smile. "Oh no thank you. I live just through the woods there."

"You mean you missed your stop?"

"Yes, yes," I admit. "That's exactly what I mean. I really must be going now."

"I could walk with you, if you like? It's sort of dangerous for a young woman all alone?"

"Thank you, no, that's very kind of you, but I'll be fine. I know the way perfectly well." And I start off down the trail where I nearly trip and fall right away. "Ohh!" I hear myself cry out.

"Hey! You okay?"

"Yes!" I call back. "Thanks! I'm fine!" I recover my footing and continue along the dark trail, pitch black, as it meanders into the woods.

'I was just too scared to accept his offer. He seemed nice enough. All the boys who worked on the trains seemed nice. But what did I know? I just wanted to be back inside the home, safe and sound. With each footstep I cursed myself for having missed the stop. What an idiot! How could you do that?

'The trail is so dim in the darkness I have a hard time seeing a foot in front of me. I nearly trip and fall several times. When I hear footsteps behind me, I stop dead in my tracks. The footsteps stop too. I thought first of the young train guy, had he followed me? Or one of the Nazi soldiers? Where'd they get off to anyway?

"Hello?" I call out behind me. "Hello?" I call again.

There is no response. Was there someone out there? The train guy? Or someone else? When no one answered I began to feel my heart pound in my chest. I start walking again. The footsteps start up again too. When I speed up, so do they. When I slow down, so do they. My heart starts beating wildly, then all of a sudden, I fall. I'd tripped on something or other. The sound of my fall echoes back and forth in the trees and I start to laugh. I realize the footsteps I heard were the echoes of my own footsteps. I am not hurt, just a bit tarnished and I pick myself up and keep going.

'A few minutes later I arrive back at the home and go in through the kitchen. There is Blum sitting at the table with a beer. He is alone.

"So! There you are, Fraulein Helga!" His voice booms.

"I'm sorry to be late Monsieur Blum." I keep my head down.

Blum reaches into his pocket and pulls out his watch. "Mmm," he says studying the timepiece. "Judging by the time, I'd say you must've missed your stop."

"Yes. I did."

"Someone gave you a lift?"

"No," I answer, too nervous to say anything more.

"What? You mean you made a hot-foot through the forest in the pitch dark of night?" And he laughs one of his giant belly shaking laughs. Then he looks at me more closely. "And you fell down too?"

"Yes. But I'm fine." I look at him now. "It was very peaceful."

"Well," he says, his amusement giving way to respect. "I didn't think you had it in you."

'That was Blum! That's how he was. Full of life! He laughed all the time. Life was amusing to him. Fooling the Nazis. Working with the Black Market to keep food coming in. Also dealing with the Resistance. Always keeping it in the context of business. He wore the mantle of "businessman", but he was a lover too. I had no doubt of that. He was the kind of man who understood power and how to manipulate people. Very attractive to women! And it was undoubtedly so with Marie Albert. Not to mention her sister.

'Marie Albert worshipped efficiency and Blum was certainly that. Yet judging by what happened later he must've shielded her from knowing certain things. Certain of his connections that caused him trouble after the war.

'The home was full of secrets and intrigues and that's what I loved most about it.'

Chapter Thirteen

Desperation Arrives!

'Only a month or so after that, I came downstairs one morning and passed by Marie Albert's office where the phone was ringing and ringing. For some reason I was reminded of my mother and our last day in Berlin. The phone had rung and rung that day too. It had been the person with the address and password for Aachen.

'Today I can see Marie Albert and Monsieur Blum standing in embrace in the alcove off the kitchen. The phone in the office continues to ring. The cook was on her break. It was Dina's day off.

'I stepped back out of the line of sight and call out, "Mademoiselle Albert! The telephone!"

Marie Albert appears an instant later. She heads for the phone. "Thank you, Helga." She slips into the office and closes the door. Blum is nosing around the kitchen.

'I hated to spoil their moment together. There were so few romantic moments for anyone in this time. They'd even tried to interest me in one of the older orphan boys. He had a slight limp like I did. Maybe they thought two people limping together was cute? Or maybe they genuinely wished for me to have someone special in that way.

'Blum unlocks one of the kitchen cupboards and pulls out a small pastry on a plate. Cook must've put it in there for him. He offers me a piece of it and I accept.

"So Fraulein Helga," he says as he hands me a plate with the pastry. "I trust you pay closer attention to your train stops these days?"

Before I can answer Marie Albert comes into the kitchen. Her face is as pale as a sheet. Blum asks, "What is it, Marie?"

"That phone call. Someone claiming to be with the Resistance-"

Blum interrupts with a name.

"No!" says Marie Albert. "It was someone I don't know, Fred." Her voice was tense. "They used the password. The current password. But what they said!" She looked over at me for some reason.

"What did they say?" asks Blum.

Marie Albert looks back to him. "They said we have about eighteen hours."

"Eighteen hours? For what?"

"To get the children out of here. All the young ones. We are to pack them up two hours before dawn and take them out to a spot in the woods. They'll be met by someone there and taken to a safe house."

Blum looks surprised. I hear myself gasp. Marie Albert looks stricken. They both seem to forget I'm there. Marie Albert says, "I don't even know if we can trust this phone call, Fred. What if it's a trick?"

"We don't really have a choice here, Marie. We have to trust our sources. We can't risk having the children taken by the Nazis."

"Isn't there someone we can call for confirmation?"

Blum shakes his head. He takes a bite of pastry. "No, I'm afraid not. The Allies must be on their way. The Nazis are pulling their bets off the table. They don't need good public relations anymore."

Marie Albert nods her head. "There is no need. Now it's round up every Jew in sight. Young and old. Man, woman or child. They warned us it would go this way, remember?"

"Damn! The Allies could be here in a month, Marie!"

"Yes! That's why the children are in danger."

Blum looks puzzled. "I just wonder why it wasn't our usual friend who called?"

Marie Albert shrugs her shoulders. "I don't know. This person had the information. And the password. That's all I know."

They both fell silent a moment.

Finally Blum says. "Okay then, we have no choice. We have to trust this call."

Marie Albert looks troubled, like I've never seen her. "At first I thought it was some business connection of yours till he spoke the password. My heart stopped."

"So, we are to wait with the children in the woods and someone will take them from there?"

Marie Albert's voice went hard. "No, Fred! That's the thing! We are to deliver the children to a designated spot and leave them. We have to leave here too. Everyone. Or risk being arrested. That's what they said."

"My God!" says Blum finally looking apprehensive. "The Allies must be advancing quickly. The Nazis are turning desperate."

"Oh God! The children will be terrified!" Marie Albert looks worried. "Everything gets much more dangerous."

"Yes, my dear. You're right. I understand now." Blum nods his head. He stands up and then seems to notice me. "Ah Helga. Please don't mention any of this to anyone. Marie Albert and I will meet with the counselors and kitchen staff. We must first try to verify this information."

"Yes sir, of course, Monsieur Blum."

'I'd never seen these two like this. They were both shaken by this phone call, I could plainly see. They spoke of the end of the war. That it was coming. But the danger was to increase, not decrease. I began to feel the fear myself, at last. Then I thought of the children. Oh God! To be left alone in the woods? That was crazy!'

'An hour later all four counselors assemble in the dining room along with Marie Albert and Monsieur Blum. I am there too. Felix is minding the children with Doctor Sonya. Blum's voice is calm, but the words shock nonetheless.

"I'm sorry to have to tell you this," he begins. "We've received word from the Resistance this morning. They've told us, this place is finished, as of tomorrow. The Nazis are coming for the children unless we act tonight. We have till just before dawn to get everyone out of here. So!" He claps his hands together. "I need you all to get ready to return to your families."

Brigitte was first to speak. "But the children? What can the Nazis hope to gain by taking the children?"

"I don't know," says Blum. "Maybe they intend to use them as shields for their escape, I really don't know." Brigitte gasps. Even the beautiful Rosa looks worried.

Marie Albert says, "I think they just want to kill every last Jew they can before they surrender."

"It's pure insanity!" says Lily, the counselor who never said anything. She didn't belong to any particular group in the home, though I knew she often sided with Dina.

Annie, the fourth counselor, sat there immobile as usual. She was like a slug. Slow and somewhat dim-witted. No one seemed to care for her very much, though she was good with the children.

"Can I stay with the children?" Brigitte begs Marie Albert.

"No, I'm sorry Brigitte," Marie Albert replies. "We've been instructed to bring the children to the upper trail in the forest there, two hours before dawn. Then we must leave them there."

"Leave them?" says Brigitte. "Leave them where?"

"I know! I know!" Blum cuts in here. "It sounds crazy. But that is what we must do."

"But Monsieur Blum," Brigitte protests. "Can you be sure about this information?"

"I understand your fear," he replies. "If it's a trick by the Gestapo, they want us to walk right into the trucks, of course. But to the best of my knowledge, this is the plan of the Resistance to save the children. We have no choice but to trust them."

Rosa speaks up. "Then there is a chance it's a trick?"

"Rosa dear," says Blum. "There is a chance of that. But we must trust the information we have at this point. We really have no choice. If it turns out to be a trick, it's the chance we have to take."

Brigitte squares her shoulders. She is visibly upset. "But we can't just take them out to the woods and leave them. We're going to take them out there and turn our backs on them? Really?"

"We can. Because we have to." Marie Albert stands firm. "We must follow our instructions. And pray."

Rosa weeps silently into an embroidered handkerchief. Brigitte too has tears in her eyes. "What about the older children, like Helga here?"

Blum says, "We must help them as best we can. Only the young ones go to the forest."

Brigitte says, "Doesn't it sound suspicious? They want us to abandon the kids out there?"

Blum starts to sound impatient. "Yes, my dear, I understand your point. But it changes nothing. The person we spoke with this morning is operating from the best information they have. He knew the proper code words. What you're suggesting is that the Gestapo may have penetrated the Resistance. But we have no proof of that. So we must do as we're told."

'The children were put to bed as usual. They were told nothing of the plan. Marie Albert reasoned they would sleep better that way. Dina had come back late last night. I'd heard her boots on the stairs and wondered how she'd taken the news.

'Around three a.m. the counselors awakened the children. They were told to dress warmly, everyone was going on an early morning hike. Some of the children were not happy about this and began to cry. Others were immediately suspicious and nervous.

'Everyone was nervous, even Marie Albert and the counselors. No one could be absolutely positive it wasn't a trap set by the Gestapo. No one, not even Monsieur Blum.

'I came down into the kitchen and found Dina making porridge at the stove. We hugged each other tightly.

"Oh Helga!" she says. "I knew we couldn't count on this to last." She sounds very frightened. "What are you going to do?"

"I don't know. I'll be all right. I'll manage somewhere."

Dina's large brown eyes narrow slightly. "The almighty Blum has lost his protection."

"At least we got the warning."

"If we can trust it?" says Dina. "I've heard the Nazis are calling everyone to the front. Everyone!"

"All those poor German boys."

"You mean stinking rotten Nazis, Helga! Who'd like to turn us both into soap."

I shudder. "Oh Dina!"

'A short time later most all the children are eating their porridge in the dining room. Rosa, Brigitte and Lily had spent the night. They were doing their best to keep the children calm.

'Marie Albert comes in and announces they have five minutes to finish their breakfast. She claps her hands once sharply. Some of the little heads snap up. Some children start to ask questions but the counselors simply tell them to hurry and eat. Brigitte and Rosa were talking in hushed whispers, but I could hear them.

"Most of her things were still there. In her room," says Rosa. "Except for the essentials, y'know?"

Brigitte nods solemnly. "Oh God, I hope they make it safely. I never figured they'd actually run for it like this."

"It was the news from yesterday, I think. Before that they were not certain." Rosa looks worried. "I told them they'd be better off here."

"Sonya didn't think so. She'd told me several times if not for the children, they'd have left before this."

I knew now for sure they were speaking of Felix and Doctor Sonya.

"Here where though?" asks Brigitte. "Could you hide them?"

Rosa shakes her head. "No. We have no place to hide anyone."

"So where were they to go?" Brigitte shakes her head. "The damn Nazis seem more worried about killing Jews than they do about losing the war."

"Poor Sonya. I know she felt as if they had no choice. Some people felt it was not an appropriate thing, those two being together."

"Felix is young. But he is mature for his age. And he adores Sonya, we know this."

'I would've been surprised, except I'd seen them leave. Together. It was sometime after midnight. I hadn't slept a wink. I'd been peeking out the bedroom window and I'd seen Felix and Doctor Sonya in the courtyard below. You could always see how much he loved her. And how excited they were to be running away together.

'Knapsacks on their backs, they'd both climbed onto Felix's bicycle and away they'd pedaled. I'd felt envious to say the least. Fleeing by myself seemed altogether meaningless. But imagine fleeing with someone you loved above everyone else? That seemed glorious! Thrilling and romantic!

'It was still pitch dark outside when we took the children out into the forest. It was the same trail through the woods I'd walked that night I'd missed my train stop. I would never forget Blum's voice when he'd told me, "I didn't think you had it in you."

'The woods themselves were not that frightening. It's really your imagination which frightens you. However this time we were all terrified about leaving the children out there alone.

'Some of the children were crying, visibly frightened, absorbing the fear from the grown-ups. Once we'd reached the start of the upper trail, we gathered the children together and told them to wait right here and someone would come for them. Marie Albert addressed the counselors sternly. She told them they were not to turn around as we left. "…Our orders were quite clear on this point. No one looks back!" Rosa and Brigitte were both holding back tears. We all walk quickly away then. We could hear some crying behind us. It was brutal! We heard nothing more. Saw nothing at all.

'Coming back inside the kitchen, Brigitte was crying openly now. "They looked so brave," she says sobbing. "Holding hands and all. I thought my heart would break in two. Crack right down the middle! Oh Rosa!"

And the two embrace. Rosa nods solemnly. "Walking away was the hardest thing I've ever had to do."

"Oh! Tell me they're safe, Rosa! Oh dear God!"

Marie Albert enters. "Okay everyone! We're locking the doors in ten minutes. Everyone! Ten minutes!" She lowers her voice. "At dawn the Nazis are going to find an empty house here. Let them arrest Dina's dormouse, the one she's been feeding crumbs to all this time."

We all look at her. We're all thinking the same thing. The children!

Marie Albert continues softly, wearily, "We have to go by what we're told. It's the system that has kept us all alive up till now. We had no choice. If we'd disobeyed and the children had been taken, how would we have lived with ourselves?" She pauses. "I don't know who came for them, but I'm sure they did. It was no trap, we have to believe that!"

"But if it was?" says Brigitte.

"If God forbid it was, then we did the best we could. They can come get us too."

'No one had anything much to say after that. We had to get ourselves out of there. Blum took me aside. First he says, "You have somewhere to go?"

I nod. "Yes, monsieur. There is a friend of my mother's."

"Good. That's very good. The money you receive from Berlin should continue to come into the post office. You should pick it up there."

I couldn't tell him that I hadn't contacted anyone. There was no time. I didn't even have a phone number. Only the name. Of a woman I'd never even met.

'Dina and I rode the first inbound train together that morning. There'd been tearful goodbyes with everyone at the home. There was never any question about me staying with Dina and her parents. They were practically starving as it was. There was no way! I could never have stood living in that tenement apartment. Huddled together like rats! I'd have preferred death by the Nazis. But then, I didn't really know what that meant.

"What are you going to do, Helga? Where will you go?"

I shrug. "I don't know, but I'll think of something. Someone will help me, I'm certain." Though I honestly had no idea who that might be at the time.

"You sound so confident, like you always do." Dina manages a half-hearted smile. "Well you know you can always come to us, in case you have a problem."

I smile back. "Don't worry, Dina. I'll be fine. You'll see, we'll all be back at Blum's after the Nazis are gone."

We left the train together. Inside the station we hugged goodbye. I suddenly wanted to be away from her. Those bedraggled boots and all. It felt as if I didn't get away, I'd somehow be forced to go with her and live in that dreadful studio apartment. With the rats!

'I hold my head up as I watch Dina walk away. I was thinking how much I missed the home already. How wonderful it'd been there! I walk into the main part of the cavernous train station. My star concealed under my handbag as always, I pass by Nazis and civilians alike. No one seems to pay any attention to me. I'm invisible! But a wave of nausea and panic starts to rise in my gut. There is a row of phone cabins each with a little seat and a folding door. I find one at the very end of the line, go inside, close the door and collapse.

'Alone in that phone booth everything catches up with me at once. Being forced to leave the home. My mother's terrible and senseless death at the hands of that idiot doctor. My father trapped in a Nazi death camp. But most of all, the end of that idyllic time at Blum's home. I'd been ridiculously happy there. Oh! How I missed them all so much! Already!

'Then too the fear finally hit me. The "displaced fear" that old Jewish couple had warned me about. Not a fear of dying in the death camps though, no! That would've been noble somehow. But my fear was a more personal thing. I was afraid of disappointing my dead mother. My poor dear angel of a mother. She'd worried and worried about me right up to her dying breath. I couldn't let them get me now, it would be like letting her down completely.

'Yet I wanted to give up! It was by far the worst moment of the whole thing for me. I sat there alone in that phone booth and cried for hours. I'd never felt so terribly alone in my whole life.

'After about two hours a name started floating around in my memory. It was a name Erna had given to my mother and me before she left. A woman: "Tedeski". Erna had said, "Call her if you get in a bad situation. I can't promise, but she might be able to help. But! Only call her as a very last resort."

'I reach for the phone directory and search for the name. There it is! I dial the number. It rings several times before a woman answers. "Hello?"

"Hello. Madame Tedeski?"

"Who is calling, please?" Her voice was nice. Cautious, but nice. I knew from the first instant she would help me. I didn't even need eye contact. I explained who I was and all that had happened, my mother dying and all. Madame Tedeski tells me to come right over to her house and she gives me the address.'

Chapter Fourteen

"We'd Love to Take Her…"

'The trolley took me out to Port Namur. The address was in one of the nicest parts of Brussels. In fact to look at the exterior of the houses, many with nice cars, one would never know a war had been raging for five years. The trees along the sidewalk were full of green leaves. Birds were singing in the branches. I began to feel hopeful.

'I rang the doorbell of Madame Tedeski's address, a swank townhouse with an ornate polished brass lion on the door. It was opened by a woman, very nicely dressed, attractive, somewhere around forty. She looked tall and sturdy with dark black hair and a warm gracious smile.

"Come in, darling girl! Come in! Helga? Did you say? How charming! One of those delightfully charming German names."

"Thank you, ma'am. Yes, if only all we Germans were as charming as our names."

"Oh my! And a sharp sense of humor too! Helga, my dear, you'll fit right in with my crowd. Your timing is divine! Tonight is the usual Thursday night card party. Just twelve or so. Nazi haters all of them!" Her tone of voice shifts. "Of course, with whom else are we to do business? I mean, people have to survive."

"Yes, they do," I agree. She asks about my circumstances. I fill her in on the closing of Blum's home and leaving the children out in the forest before dawn.

"Oh my God, dear child!" Madame Tedeski cries. "I'm so sorry! It must've been torture for you this whole business. On top of losing your poor dear mother. Come on into the kitchen, let's have something to eat."

'Madame Tedeski welcomes me into her home as if I were her own family. We eat together as we arrange food on platters for her guests tonight. My eyes could hardly believe the food she had in the house. Cream cheese and caviar. Smoked salmon and steak tartare! Now I understood her remark about with whom you do business. Nazis had the money. I wondered what sort of people would show up tonight.

'Madame dressed in fashionable casual elegance as she received her equally well attired guests. They arrive in small discreet clusters. She greets them warmly and immediately introduces each of them with the explanation, "We're trying to locate a suitable safe place for Helga to stay until the liberation."

'I shake all their hands and even receive a few hugs. All Madame's guests positively gush over me.

'One woman clutches her husband's arm. "Oh dear, she can come stay with us! In the guest room. Robert, darling, we're taking this sweet girl home with us tonight." She hugs me tightly. "What a darling girl you are!"

'The next couple fawned even more. "Oh, but you must let us take dear Helga home. How wonderful!" She glanced around. "You never know what you'll find at Madame Tedeski's." This woman has a shrill false-sounding laugh.

'Of course I was stunned. Nearly every single guest or couple swore on arrival they'd love to have me come stay with them. One after another! They smile and speak so generously, I immediately think, my God, we could've brought the children out here and each one of these people could've gone home with someone. Who were these people?

'Madame and her guests proceed to eat and play cards at several tables for several hours. They graze on outrageous delicacies from time to time all laid out on an ornate buffet. I helped the maid replenish items as needed.

"Darling?" cries one guest. "Where on earth did you find *fois gras*? There happens to be a war on, in case it's escaped you?" Several people laugh and clap. Some sound overly loud and tipsy.

"You mustn't ask where she gets the stuff, silly! That's the rule!" More laughter erupts. "Suffice to say our friend is connected at the highest levels."

"You'll be glad you don't know," says another guest. "Once the Nazis are gone that sort of knowledge could land you in jail."

'They laughed, ate, drank and played till almost midnight, as if there were no curfew, like it didn't apply out here. I heard several guests speak of Erna's beau Harry. That's how Erna had known about Madame Tedeski, Harry had been a regular out here. I thought how perfectly Harry would've fit in with these people. Not just Harry. But my parents and my Uncle Erich too. They would've all felt right at home with these people. I felt right at home with them too.

'As the party breaks up I stand by the door with Madame. She asks that first couple, "Shall I bring Helga over tomorrow?" This was the first couple who'd been so insistent.

The woman leans in and lowers her voice, "Oh damn! Robert reminded me about our live-in maid, Hildegard. She's a sympathizer, I'm afraid. Loves the bloody Huns! Nazi boyfriend and all. You know we'd love to take you Helga, you're so sweet! But if that damn maid were to speak to the wrong people-" She broke it off there.

Madame Tedeski nods, "Of course darling, we understand. Don't worry."

The woman looks me in the eye. "I'm so sorry, my dear. It wouldn't be safe."

'One by one each of the guests begs off their initial offer to take me in. It was another shock to my system. Each one who'd been so anxious to have me, suddenly remembered a relative or an employee which made it impossible. I'd been breathing so easily since I'd entered her house. She'd been so confident one of these people would come through for me. They'd practically been squabbling amongst themselves as to who would get to take me.

'Then to stand there and hear all their excuses, it was amazing. Everyone had a cousin or an uncle or a servant they couldn't trust. All the warm generous spirit from the start of the evening seemed to evaporate in the face of cold fear.

'Madame and I carry the glasses and plates back into the kitchen after everyone has left.

"Don't worry Helga. I have many more friends than you met tonight. I shall make some calls in the morning. Now don't worry." She sounded as confident as she had before.

"I'm just sorry to be a burden to you. I mean, a total stranger appears on your doorstep?"

"Nonsense! We're all strangers till we look each other in the eye, right? Don't worry, my sweet child, we'll hide you someplace till the Allies get here."

'The next morning Madame Tedeski had already found someone by the time I had eaten a lovely breakfast. After that we rode the trolley together about two kilometers over to Square Coghen. Number 20, is a lovely house on a beautiful cul-de-sac. A maid answers the door.

'I could hardly believe this woman still had a maid at this point in the war. The house was impeccably maintained, the shelves full of bone china and crystal glassware. One whole shelf held champagne glasses alone.

'It all belonged to a Madame Berrault. Once the maid got us settled in the living room Madame Berrault appeared carrying a tray of chocolate bread sandwiches, like the ones Henne Brotmann used to bring me at the home.

'This woman too had food and plenty of it. From the lunch she served us, you'd never guess there'd been rationing for years. All you saw and heard was about how there was no food anywhere in the country.' Helga laughs.

'I'd fallen right into the cream. Madame Berrault, she gives me a lovely bedroom upstairs across the hall from the maid's room. All of us were as cozy as bedbugs in that house for some weeks. She was wonderful! Very stylish, a woman of about thirty. Generous and kind-hearted. She had two little boys of her own, who were off safe with their father somewhere.

'About five weeks later, still wearing my now well-worn topcoat with the dreary yellow star concealed under my handbag, I left the house one morning very excited. Under my arm was tucked this beautiful white fur blanket.

'Madame Berrault had given it to me, this gorgeous blanket, soft white fur on one side and a deep red satin on the other side. I adored it! And she'd said with my sewing knowledge I could probably turn it into a lovely coat. She was right. But I needed some help and she'd directed me towards a little tailor shop just a few blocks away. Even though Madame did not like me leaving the house for any reason at all.

'It was a beautiful day in September. We'd been hearing on the radio for weeks that the Allies would be in Brussels any day. Today the streets seem unusually quiet. Empty of the usual soldiers. I am encouraged. Then I rounded the corner of the nearby main boulevard. Before I could even react a group of twenty soldiers came running towards me. I froze, completely startled as they bore down on me.

'My yellow star is only half-hidden. I realize this with a slight panic and try to move the handbag over to conceal it all the way. Only then when I look up at the last instant do I realize the soldiers are American, not German. They pass me by like I'm not even there.

'When I see they are Americans, I feel a moment's relief, followed by a much stronger wave of fear that I might be caught up in a street battle of some kind. But as quickly as they appeared, they were gone, having disappeared down one of the small side streets.

'I stood there staring after them a moment. Still I pressed my handbag tightly over the star. It was an ingrained reflex by this time. Still it occurs to me right away, if the Americans are here, it's the end of this damned yellow star business. Passing a shop window I caught sight of my own reflection in the glass. Handbag or no, there was the ugly star!

'I started to tear at the star ripping at the threads my mother had sewn. In the act of tearing it off I look up and now see eight or ten Nazi soldiers running right at me. They are all armed and look quite panicked. Again I freeze, my hand holding the half-torn star in place.

'Eight of the ten Nazis run past me, and they keep running down the sidewalk. But two of them stop. One points his pistol at me. "Hey Otto!" he calls to his friend. "Look here at this one!" Then he looks at me. "So? You are tired of wearing your star, my pretty little Yid?"

The other Nazi stops to look, but he keeps hopping about nervously. "Come on, Johann! Shoot her and be done with it!"

I stood there stiff with fear. A long moment passes. The soldier and I look at each other steadily. There was the sudden sound of bootsteps on pavement. The Nazi pulls up his pistol.

"What's the matter with you?" shouts the nervous comrade. "You want me to shoot her for you? Come on!"

"No, no! To hell with it! Come on, Otto!" And he grabs his buddy's arm as they take off down the sidewalk.

'The Nazis ran for their lives that day. Almost all of them! They ran straight out of town. Except for certain groups of them who would stop and make a futile stand at one particular street corner or another. They would plant a machine gun or two on the ground and start blasting away indiscriminately, firing at everything and nothing. They were in desperation now.

'We all ran that day. I ran too. I never ran so hard as I did that day. By the next day it was all over. The remaining Nazis fled the city overnight. Like rats, they vanished! We saw a few of them, their clothes and uniforms now torn, dirty and ragged. They were scorned and harassed along the way.

Chapter Fifteen

A Strange End Sensation

'The next morning the town of Brussels poured out into the streets. They are hugging and kissing and dancing! They are drinking and getting drunk, from early in the day until late at night. Everyone was dancing. They played music in the streets. The entire town of Brussels it seems now, suddenly moves out into the street to celebrate. Men, women and children.

'I myself would stay wrapped up in that white fur blanket with the red satin lining. I wore it like a shawl around my shoulders as I went all over around the city. Everyone kept to the streets for days. The whole town was delirious with joy.

'The entire city seemed to be partying in the streets. There was food and drink galore! I myself am in the middle of it, though somehow at the same time I feel invisible. People smile at me, and a stranger or two stops to embrace me. They all say how they love my red satin wrap. Still there is no one to really connect with.

'There is no one to search out exactly. I don't know for sure where my cousin Bernie lives now. There is no one searching me out in particular. I'm consumed by a curiosity about the children from Blum's home. Are they safe? I had no way to know, as of yet.

'I was happy to see everyone so happy, of course! The Nazis were gone, and all that wicked fear, they took it along with them. Still somehow try as I might, and I did try very hard, I couldn't quite find the same level of wild exuberance that I saw all around me. At one point a young man near my age grabs me by the shoulders and plants a big kiss on my lips before he offers me a sip of champagne from the bottle. I take a sip and the young man moves on to another girl.

'I feel a sudden ache for my mother. A genuine pain! Why wasn't she here? And my father! Where was he now? Would he be liberated too? Or was he already dead? The questions only made for more pain!

'The more joy I saw in everyone, the people so filled with joy, the more empty I began to feel. So terribly empty. As if someone had given me my life back, but it was now stripped of everything meaningful and important. It was now a life without heart or soul. This feeling, though I fought against it, would persist inside me for a long time.

'I left Madame Berrault's house a few days later. Madame Tedeski was there as well. The ladies gave me a bag full of goodies to take back to the home. Celebrations in the street had calmed only just slightly. The city of Brussels was still quite delirious with joy.

"Helga darling," says Madame Berrault. "Are you sure you won't reconsider and stay on with us. You don't need to return to that orphanage of Blum's. We can help you get settled in with a job of some sort."

Madame Tedeski nods vigorously. "You can come back here if it doesn't work out."

"Thank you!" I say. "You've been so generous to me. Both of you! Where would I be now, if you both hadn't helped me? I wouldn't have made it through." They both hug me and kiss my cheek. "The home is still my home for now. I have a proper place there and I am useful in the household. Besides that, I must find out what happened with the children. The ones we left alone in the woods that day. I still have no idea."

"Of course, of course." The ladies look at each other a moment. "Please come back and tell us too."

'I promise I will return to visit. A few months later Erna will return to Brussels and she will insist on taking me under her wing for a time. She had another man now. Nothing like Harry. The story Erna had heard was that Harry had killed himself in a Nazi transit camp. Her new man was nice. And wealthy too.

They begged me to come with them on a trip to Monte Carlo. I did too. But all this was much later. At the moment I needed to return to Blum's home because the only heart I really knew was there. With Marie Albert. And Dina. Blum himself and all of them.'

'I took the trolley out to Wezembeek Oppem just like I had during the occupation. It seemed much the same. Allied soldiers had replaced the Nazis. They were crude as well, but in a harmless way.

'Arriving at the home I knocked on the side door by the kitchen and was greeted warmly by Marie Albert. We embraced for a moment.

"Helga dear! How wonderful to see you! You look well. You didn't suffer too badly these last few weeks?" She was genuinely pleased to see me, I could tell.

"Oh not at all, Mademoiselle Albert. I was well taken care of by a sweet lady. A Madame Tedeski. And her friend Madame Berrault."

Marie Albert nods thoughtfully. Had she heard of these women? I didn't know and couldn't ask. Marie Albert still frightened me a little. Those eyes of hers! She could turn them on you and you froze.

"Were the children saved? After we left them in the forest?"

"Oh yes, my dear. The warning we received was genuine. A resistance worker took them to a safe hiding place."

Brigitte the counselor came in the kitchen and she trilled, "Helga! Sweet girl! You're all right!" And she comes over to hug me.

I looked at them both. "Do you know if the death camps have been liberated?"

Marie Albert shakes her head no. "Monsieur Blum says the war still goes on to the east. From all reports the death camps are carrying on with their gruesome campaign."

Brigitte says, "But the war is lost for Germans, Mademoiselle Marie. Why persist in killing Jews?"

I was upset too. "Why don't the Americans bomb the train tracks leading to the death camps? They could stop the deportations!"

Marie Albert looks sympathetic. "I suppose they must save their bombs for more strategic targets."

I slumped. "But they have plenty of bombs. My poor father!"

Blum suddenly enters the kitchen. "Hello dear Helga! How wonderful to see you!" He comes up and gives me a quick embrace. He then turns to the others. His tone of voice goes serious. "I've just gotten word. Our two friends did not make it. They were both arrested at the border into Luxembourg. Taken to a camp. Both of them."

Brigitte cries. "Oh dear God! Poor Sonya!"

"Oh no! Doctor Sonya? And Felix? Oh how terrible!"

"Yes," says Brigitte. "They should've stayed put here! They could've survived."

'The core people came back to the home in Wezembeek for a time. Marie Albert would be able to keep it going for a year or so. She and Alfred Blum would be married in 1945. But by then, I'd begun to make a sort of life for myself in Brussels.

'I heard that charges of collaboration were brought against Monsieur Blum. But to the best of my knowledge he was never actually brought to trial.'

(Editor's note: Given the tenuous nature of the Jewish Councils, the AJB, and Blum's role as treasurer and secretary there in Brussels, it was reasonable to expect the anger of both the Jewish Resistance and the Communists after the war. They continued to believe that Blum and the AJB had cooperated far too much during the occupation. That they'd compiled lists of names and addresses and issued "registration cards" etc., all allowing the Nazis to keep track of the still free Jewish population. In fact the Jewish Council had adopted an official policy of "lesser evil", which made apparent submission look somewhat like collaboration. It was actually just survival.

The fact that Blum himself had been arrested in September of 1942 and held for two weeks, nearly shipped off to Auschwitz along with other AJB directors did not help. The very fact that he'd been released and then allowed to keep his orphanages and old folks homes operating caused suspicion. However, though charges were made and filed. There is no record of any actual trials for any of the AJB people taking place. Not so for all non-Jewish citizens of Brussels.)

Helga tells us, 'Marie Albert was considered above any sort of collaboration. She was never suspected. She was above reproach from that standpoint. Madame Tedeski, Erna and Harry's friend, who'd first helped that terrible day I'd had to leave the home, was not bothered. She'd run that private card game in her beautiful home in Port Namur, but somehow did not come under scrutiny.

'However her friend Madame Berrault, with whom I stayed the last weeks before liberation. Who'd fed me bread and chocolate and lovely cold cuts! She was put on trial and found guilty of Black Market offences. She even went to jail briefly. I don't know for how long, but this was how it was afterwards. Anyone who had survived in too much style or comfort was brought under suspicion.

'Blum himself might've come under more pressure if not for Marie Albert. The International Red Cross stood in total awe of Marie Albert. If anyone in Brussels applied for work with the recommendation of Marie Albert, they were hired on the spot.

'I have no memory of seeing Dina again, though it's possible I did. She had never been terribly fond of Blum or Marie Albert. Maybe she agreed with those who thought Blum hadn't resisted hard enough? I'd thought she wanted to know about my father, whose last letter was postmarked "Thereisenstadt" a Nazi deportation camp somewhere near Czecholslovakia. He wrote again how he hoped I continued with my studies. That he was sure I was a fine upstanding young woman. Also that I might become a doctor, because it was a fine life dedicated helping people.

'My father never returned. I had no idea what had happened to him until many months after the Nazi surrender. I received a letter from an elderly couple who had been inmates along with my father at the camp Theriesenstadt.

'It read: "We know you don't know who we are, dear Helga, but we are obliged to write you this letter about your dear father, Hans Wallnau. We hope and pray that this letter finds you alive and well. We were privileged to know your father and we want you to know what an inspiration he was to us and everyone inside the camp. Your father was a continuous shining light of good humor, kindness and hope for all of us in the camp. We are not certain but it's quite possible your dear father did not survive until liberation. And in that light we needed to write this letter to you in hopes you have survived and that you know what a great man your father was. He was forever cheerful, even brightening the spirits of those headed to the gas chamber. Your father Hans will always and forever remain first in our prayers."

'I never saw my father again. Years later I heard many stories of Jews in the camps who had saved themselves one way or another. My father could tailor clothes and he played piano at a professional level. He could've saved himself, I'm sure. But he wasn't that sort of man. He was too Prussian. I'm sure he would've considered entertaining Nazis a fate worse than death. He was an idealist. A proud Prussian and a dreamer too.

'Uncle Erich, he was the practical one. He left Germany early and made a new life for himself and Aunt Molly in New York. He was a success all over again. My father died in the camps. Erich died in a nursing home.' Helga laughs abruptly. 'The irony of life. If I remember right, he had a touch of dementia, but he outlived his own doctor. That was a great source of pride. He said, his doctor always told him not to smoke cigars or eat this or that. Erich loved it that he out-lived that doctor.

'I stayed on there in Brussels, Belgium for over a year. I had no thoughts of returning to Berlin. I felt like there was nothing there for me anymore. I found some decent employment and I enjoyed the company of some of my mother's friends. We went out dating and night-clubbing. Yet still I was plagued by tremendous feelings of emptiness. I longed for a life that had not been stripped of meaning and importance. I suppose for me that meant my family. I managed to contact my Uncle Erich in New York and he sent me a ticket for boat passage. He wrote that he and Aunt Molly would act as my sponsors.

'I had learned the basics of taking X-ray photographs of hospital patients and I worked for a doctor there in Brussels. When I told him I was leaving to go live in America he told me, "My dear, it is not who you are for which you're responsible, it is the impression you leave behind". It was a little thing but somehow I would never forget it.'

Above: Helga Wallnau Burch (circa 1986)

Epilogue

Editor's note: The following information was found online.

Yona Tiefenbrunner, (and wife Ruth) at whose home in Brussels Helga stayed briefly before moving out to Wezembeek Oppem, was considered a big hero by the Belgian Jewish resistance. Yona undoubtedly saved many Jewish children from the 'final solution'. One story told by his eyewitness friend says that Yona called him one day and asked if the friend could help him with an errand. Yona said he was going to the Gestapo office to try and save a young Jewish boy who'd been taken into custody.

"I'm sure I can get him released into my care, but I need someone to come along in case I'm taken and arrested myself." Yona Tiefenbrunner was a designated custodian of orphan Jewish children with parents who had been deported.

"What can I do?" asked the friend.

"I want you to wait on the street corner where you can see the front entrance to the Gestapo. You wait exactly one-half hour. If I don't come out by then, you must return to the home and tell them. Alert Alfred Blum as well."

The friend agreed and the two set off. At the corner where he stationed his friend, Yona took off his gold watch and asked his friend to hold it while he was gone. The friend took the watch and watched Yona walk right into the Gestapo police station. "It was the longest half-hour of my life, waiting like that," says the friend. "Right at the last minute Yona came out with the boy."

The friend who tells the story to an online Jewish magazine is every bit as astonished by the result as he was by Tiefenbrunner's courage. It is also further proof that Alfred Blum and the Jewish Council of Brussels were instrumental in the survival of the Jewish orphans in Brussels.

It's also vital to understand that a deal had been struck with the Nazis on the surface. A bargain that was sanctioned and defended by the Belgian royal family and emissaries of the Vatican. That deal said that children whose parents had been deported, i.e. sent to Auschwitz, would not face deportation themselves. The Nazis would break this deal, but they would also end up honoring it more than once, simply for benefit of public relations. The other part of the bargain said that Jews born in Belgium would be exempt from the round-ups. This accounts for some of the confusion at the round-up from which Helga had a very narrow escape. Presumably if you could show proof you were born in Belgium you had some shred of hope.

Elsewhere on the web we found several accounts involving the separate arrests of both Marie Albert and Alfred Blum by the Nazis during the occupation.

We believe these arrests occurred while Helga was staying at the Tiefenbrunner home, since the home in Wezembeek was the site of the arrest of Marie Albert. Only two months after being given funds and permission to open the orphanage, the Nazis invade the home and arrest Marie Albert and sixty children. This is the afternoon of Oct 30, 1942. The account says one of the counselors took off through the backyard and into the woods and was never seen again. It goes on to say that the Nazis were allowing any non-Jews who worked there to be paid off and let go. As Marie Albert was paying one Julia Davis, Marie slipped her a note with the telephone of the Tiefenbrunners and said, "Call now and say, 'Child welfare'!"

According to this account Marie Albert and the children were then put in a transport and driven to a transit camp. Julia Davis telephones Yona Tiefenbrunner, who in turn calls one Yvonne Nevejean, who is known to be friendly with Belgium's Queen Elisabeth.

It is a mere twenty-four hours before the Belgian Queen is petitioning the Nazi commandant and enlisting the aid of Cardinal Roey. Marie Albert and 58 children were released the next day. In addition to the children from the home, Marie Albert is credited with "grabbing" at least one other young boy being held at the transit camp. They are all allowed to return to Wezembeek.

Another online account tells of the arrest of Alfred Blum and five other directors of the Belgian Jewish Councils. This happened in late September of 1942, a month before the raid on the home in Wezembeek. Those arrested including Alfred Blum were the upper echelon of the Jewish elite in Brussels. These six men who'd been taken into custody from the offices of the Jewish Council were then transported to a transit camp from where thousands and thousands of Jews were deported, all under the auspices of Nazi "work orders". In order to fill a quota set by Berlin, the Occupational Nazi Forces in Belgium would start round-ups and frequently ignore the provisions of the exemption agreement.

Blum and the others are held for two weeks at the transit camp before the intervention of Queen Elisabeth and Cardinal Van Roey. It is at this point around October of 1942, that the internal differences between levels of occupying Nazis seems to have broken out and come into play. It is the more militaristic Nazi elements who favor simply arresting every Jew they find, while the more political levels favor holding onto a semblance of legitimate governance.

The political elements hold sway in the fight. Thus Alfred Blum and the Jewish Council after their release from custody are charged with the maintenance of the Jewish orphanages and several old folks homes. The AJB as the Council was called would operate and do their best to save Jewish lives until the very last day of occupation in Brussels.

According to records, the home at Wezembeek Oppem was not raided again until August of 1944, which would jibe with Helga's account of Blum and Marie Albert closing the home completely on just twelve hours notice. That being the morning they escort the children into the woods where they were told to leave them.

While we found no such "inauguration" of Alfred Blum's gravestone, we did find online pictures of a ceremony at Brussels' Etterbeek cemetery in 2002 for the inauguration of Marie Albert Blum's gravestone. The ceremony was attended by eight survivors of the Nazi time, who lived under the protection and direction of Marie Albert at the home in Wezembeek, including four who had been arrested with her in October of '42.

Sadly Marie Albert had died a year before this commemoration in 2001 at age 86. This was four years after the publication of her book "Un Recif d'Espoir, (Reef of Hope) Memories of War in a Jewish Children's Home" in 1997.

Editor's Postscript:

Helga arrived in the United States at Port of New York in 1948. She was sponsored by her uncle Erich Oling.

Through her uncle's business connections she briefly dated Greek royal George Papadoupalous. However she ended up marrying Sydney Burch in 1950. Helga continued working as an X-ray technician on the East Coast. She and Sydney were blessed with two sons and eventually emigrated to the West Coast and the Monterey Peninsula, where Sydney taught high school and Helga went on to earn a degree in Marriage and Family Counseling.

Helga lost her beloved Sydney in 1984. She continued to work in the Counseling field on the Central Coast.

For some years Helga made numerous visits to local grade schools to tell of her Holocaust experiences.

At 97 years of age Helga Wallnau Burch survives to this day. She lives in a skilled nursing facility in the Monterey area. Although her ability to recall much of her story escapes her these days. She says, "It's up to you, Jeffrey. To help them remember my story. That's why I told it to you, my friend."

I invite all dear readers to join me in spreading Helga's story, the timeless testimony of one brave teenager's survival amidst a genocidal nightmare.

A society divides against itself, then tries to conquer the world. Fear of arrest, betrayal and discovery keep most citizens paralyzed. However a certain few resist and fight against racial genocide, against a fatally flawed monocultural ethic, against a totalitarian autocracy worshipping a single man. As a pure innocent Helga represents youth marginalized by prejudice. It is in the nature of her "survival points" to act as a mirror for ourselves. Her story challenges each and every one of us to stand up for all victims of blind prejudice in whatever society we live.

Helga and I discussed many things during our sessions besides the details of her adolescent history evading Nazi capture. Over the course of her adult studies in Psychology and while acquiring her license to practice Marriage and Family Counseling, Helga developed a line of therapy all her own. Certainly influenced by her experiences, Helga's theory was based on the "client's fantasies". As a therapist Helga believed a great many people suffered from a sort of "fantasy deprivation", that is, the inability to make lifelong fantasies even those developed during childhood come true.

"Tell me your deepest fantasies. And we will go from there," Helga would say.

"We are ruled by our fantasies." Her sessions with clients involved deep explorations of the origins and meanings of the client's imaginations, i.e. whom they would love and marry, what sort of career they would thrive in, and the expectations of friends and family.

In the years since I interviewed Helga, I've come to a deeper understanding of this "fantasy therapy" approach. I believe Helga's intuitive understanding of how important our fantasies are to our overall mental health is a unique and vital approach to helping fight neurosis. Or even psychosis. The Nazis acted inhumanely under what was possibly a mass neurotic fantasy, namely that Jews were responsible for all society's ills. This sort of delusion persists to this day. It makes Helga's story and her perceptions all the more vital and critical for us today.

Around the time of our sessions Helga enjoyed a book called "The Reader" about a man who discovers that his first love had been a Nazi guard at a death camp. We were both intrigued by the question of whether someone can love a person who has committed unspeakable crimes.

"It's all about the heart," says Helga. "Real love is always between the two hearts, when it's genuine. The heart has no memory or knowledge of the past. The heart knows only the present moment. Of course you can love someone who's possibly done great evil. Because evil is a notion of the brain and the intellect. The heart knows nothing of those things."

"That reminds me of Hannah Arendt and her 'Eichmann in Jerusalem' piece. "'The banality of evil' was her phrase. She contended that he killed Jews because that was his job. That he was not capable of hating them in his heart."

"I agree with her," says Helga. "Although it's difficult to imagine that he could ever be fond of a Jew. Remember my father when he found his cousin in the phone book?" Helga laughs. "'What!' The man said, 'You're a dirty Jew? Don't ever call me again!'" And she laughs again.

"How can you laugh?" I ask.

"Oh! Only because I remember my father and his surprise. He was such a dreamer, my father."

"But your father is the great hero of the story for me. That letter from those people in the camp with him. That's the highest praise a human being can earn."

Helga's temper flashes. "What do you know? You don't know anything! My father died in the camps. Uncle Erich! He was the hero. He saved himself and his family. And others too." She pauses. "My father kept saying, 'Hitler can't last'."

I nod my head. Her feelings are understandable. If Hans Wallnau had listened to his brother-in-law, they might've all survived, instead of just Helga. "The hardest thing for me to get is how people watched their neighbors being taken away. People they'd known their whole lives. Taken away because of their ancestry."

Helga is calm again. "Come on now, Jeffrey. We know if you knew the right people and had the money, your heritage could be 'fixed'."

"Of course, of course," I say. "It's like how many members of Congress have sons fighting in Iraq?"

"Exactly!" says Helga. "Arabs in America are like the Jews. Or Muslims rather. Bush doesn't care how many die for his cause. Look at the pictures from that prison over there! How they torture and humiliate the Iraqi prisoners."

"You mean they treat them like animals, because the U.S. soldiers have been indoctrinated to think of them as no better than animals. Ragheads!"

"Just like they did with the Jews in Germany," says Helga.

"For sure. Once the official state policy is 'To hate and kill all Jews', if you don't hate and kill Jews, you're unpatriotic. It's amazing how we human beings keep making the same mistakes over and over."

"It's all fear, Jeffrey. Or at least it's based in fear. Maybe Hitler did actually fear that his grandfather had been Jewish? Maybe that was the seed of his hatred?"

"I can understand that. Because the Jewish tendency is to question authority. That is anathema to a fascist. I can see Hitler being terrified he had some Jewish blood in him. Turning that terror to blind hatred is a short step."

Helga nods. "They will always love Hitler! Those people! He came from nothing. How many times did he escape being killed? It was amazing! They will blame the others, Himmler and

Goebbels and Eichmann. But Hitler they will celebrate. He was purifying the German race."

"What a joke! Racial purity is a road to extinction. It's the diversity which keeps a race healthy and able to fight off disease."

"That's the human condition. People usually want what's bad for them."

I laugh. "Like the story of Adam and Eve, the snake and the apple?"

Helga laughs. "Yes, of course! And who do they blame? The innocent snake!"

"Yes! And Eve too. They always blame Eve."

"Yes of course. That's like blaming Jews."

"So?" I say. "What is the great lesson of the Nazi time? That there is no real truth? No real lies? It's simply whatever the people believe at the time."

"That's true. That is one lesson."

"That people will watch their neighbors being hauled off to death camps for no real reason."

"Yes," says Helga. "And as long as they believe they won't be next."

"There are an infinite number of lessons I suppose."

"The same lesson we must keep learning over and over."

"What's that?" I ask.

A twinkle returns to Helga's eyes. "The more you're sure you're right, the greater the chance you're wrong."

I laughed. "Of course, of course. Like those neo-Nazis I saw in Avignon last spring. But isn't there a lesson about looking for someone else to do your thinking for you? The surrender of reason and logic?"

Her eyes twinkle even more. "You mean in the Talmudic sense?"

"Yes! Yes! The Jewish tradition of questioning everything? I believe that lies at the crux of it all."

Helga laughs. "You're right. But people still believe there are no poor Jews. Jews without money. They believe all Jews are rich."

We laughed together. Helga had never lost her sense of humor. She loved to laugh. She loved people. And she loved life.

**In the early 1990's Helga Wallnau Burch was invited to visit the National Holocaust Archives in Washington, D.C. and record part of her story.

As mentioned before Helga Wallnau Burch is an award-winning poet. Below is one of her poems of which she is most proud.

Life Sounds
By Helga Wallnau Burch

I listen to the night/
    And hear the pain/
        Beyond the silence.
I listen to the night/
    And hear life's violence.
I listen to the night/
    And hear the stars.
I listen to the night/
    And hear no wars.
I listen to the night/
    And hear rain hit the ground.
I listen.
I listen to the night/
    And beyond night's dark silence,
        I can hear life's sound.

Made in the USA
Middletown, DE
20 March 2023